TEARS IN A BOTTLE
COMFORT FOR LIFE'S HURTS

To Helen & Howard,

by
Noah Martin

*May God bless you
and keep you in His
love & care*

Noah Martin

TEARS IN A BOTTLE

COMFORT FOR LIFE'S HURTS

Noah Martin

NOAH'S ARK PUBLISHING CO.

ISBN 0-9700373-0-9

Library of Congress Control Number: 00-091030

COVER DESIGN AND ILLUSTRATIONS

by

JANICE SANDAK

Published by
Noah's Ark Publishing Co.
614 Freedom Avenue
Johnstown, PA 15904

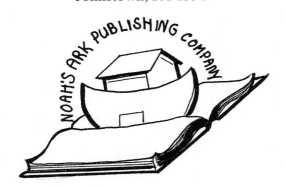

Note on Use of Scripture:

Unless otherwise noted, Scripture passages are taken from the New International Version, Copyright © 1973, 1978, 1984 by the International Bible Society

Also cited:

The Holy Bible, New King James Version (NKJV). Copyright © 1979, 1980, 1982 by Thomas Nelson, Inc., Nashville, TN

Revised Standard Version (RSV). Copyright © 1946, 1952, and 1971 by the Division of Christian Education, National Council of Churches

The Living Bible Paraphrased (TLB). Copyright © 1971 by Tyndale House Publishers

Note on Case Histories:

Numerous case histories are presented in this book. In each case, names, times, and places have been changed to protect the identities of any particular individual(s).

TABLE OF CONTENTS

ACKNOWLEDGMENTS

Sincere appreciation is expressed to —

*Dr. Catharine B. Kloss, Associate Professor of English at the University of Pittsburgh at Johnstown, for providing basic editorial skills as she worked with the style and content of the book. Most of all, I appreciated her personal encouragement.

*Betty Rosian of Words for All Reasons for offering her skills and insights as an author and editor. She offered many good ideas to improve the clarity of the book. I appreciated her persistence for details and her encouragement to complete the project.

*Craig Stoner, a staff assistant at New Day, Inc. and my good brother in the Lord, for proofreading the manuscript and assisting in providing accuracy for the biblical accounts and illustrations used.

*Rev. David McGee, pastor, hospital chaplain, grief counselor, hospice trainer, and my personal friend, who read the manuscript and offered many helpful suggestions from his work with grief-stricken individuals and families.

*Dr. Hubert Callihan and **Charlie Smith** for their invaluable help teaching me word processing on a new desktop publisher. I could never have made it without their kindness, patience, and encouragement.

*the many brave people who have shared their stories of pain and brokenness with me, either in a counseling setting or in some other way. I have learned much from their struggles to survive, their courageous efforts to find meaning in their experiences, their persistent searches to find hope in the midst of pain, and their ceaseless cries to know the comfort of God. They have helped me to face my own painful times and to join their search to find hope. I've learned the greatest lessons of life and faith from those who have suffered much.

"Out of suffering have emerged the strongest souls, and the most massive characters are seamed with scars."
—Edwin Hubbell Chaplin

X

TEARS IN A BOTTLE

You have seen me tossing and turning

through the night.

You have collected all my tears

and preserved them in your bottle!

You have recorded every one in your book.

— **Psalm 56:8 (TLB)**

TEARS IN A BOTTLE

INTRODUCTION

Life can be painful—so very, very painful. The pains of life can come as jolts that hit you unprepared, or they can come as slow, unrelenting poundings over the years. But you cannot escape pain or problems in this life. Everyone hurts sometimes.

Life is filled with many tragedies, disappointments, losses, and changes, from a child's loss of a pet to a major natural catastrophe in which thousands of lives are lost. Life is uncertain and beset with many dangers. You don't usually stop to think about how painful life is until you experience pain for yourself or someone close to you is stricken. Then the reality sets in—you, too, are vulnerable.

Many painful times are associated with losses. The loss of anything you value causes pain. The death of a loved one is one of the most obvious of the painful losses. But there are many other losses you grieve as well. The ending of a relationship is also a very painful loss, whether it comes through separation, divorce, or the breaking off of a meaningful friendship. You respond with sorrow and grief for that special loved one.

You also grieve through many of life's natural changes in relationships, family structures, employment, aging, leaving familiar places, and moving on. It seems as if you are always saying "good-bye" to someone or something. While these changes are not necessarily bad, you often grieve as they occur. An empty sadness fills your heart. It hurts to let go of what you have to face the uncertainty of change. There are many losses for which Hallmark does not make a card.

This book is born out of my own acquaintance with emotional pain and the many years of working with people in pain—hurting and troubled people, broken families, people who have experienced major tragedies and losses, people lost and alone in depression. Dealing with my own pain has helped me to understand the deep pain of others. But I have also experienced "moments of grace" that sustained me through the painful times. God has promised to be faithful, and He is.

In this book, I will offer you ways to face, express, and deal with the pains that life brings. I cannot answer the question "Why?", but I will offer hope as you face painful times. I will identify spiritual and emotional resources as lights in the darkness and anchors of the soul that will help you find your way through pain. In particular, I pray that you will be able to draw great spiritual strength from the ways Christ dealt with His pain.

You can deal with pain; you can move through it and beyond it; you can experience "moments of grace" that will sustain you; you can find the comforting presence of God; you can find strength to endure and hope to press on; and, amazingly, you can discover that pain will even help you to grow. As Bob Savino has written in "Song of the Floating Worlds":

"Nothing is lost. All we have suffered frames
a teaching for the soul."

-------------- **SECTION 1** --------------

INNER PAIN DEFINED

CHAPTER 1

DESCRIPTIONS OF PAIN

Emotional pain is a response to a significant loss, disappointment, hurt, fear, or failure. Something meaningful has been taken away or something you wanted very badly has been denied. You feel that the loss can never be recovered. You long for that which is not. An intense sense of loss leads to pain and grief, which you feel as a deep, inner aching of the soul, an emptiness that is yearning to be filled. If you are in emotional pain right now, you know all too well how it feels.

I've heard pain described in these ways:

"It feels like a cement truck ran right through the middle of my gut."

"It feels like my heart is breaking."

"It feels like my insides just collapsed."

"I'm in a daze. I really don't know what is happening."

"It hurts so bad I think I can reach in there and pull it out."

"It feels like someone reached in and just crushed my heart."

"I am in torment within, my heart is poured out on the ground . . ." (Lamentations 2:11)

"I feel like I'm choking. There's a tightness in my chest."

"I feel like I died and went to my own funeral."

"I'm watching myself in slow motion from a distance."

"My heart is wounded within me." (Psalm109:22)

A little girl described the pain of her grandmother's death: "It feels like a tire went flat in my stomach."

During the painful times, you often feel brokenhearted, crushed in spirit, sad, and alone. The safe and kind world you had hoped for has been torn apart. You feel violated by forces you cannot control. You feel that life is unraveling around you as you helplessly stand by. You have a sinking feeling that life is draining out of you. You are preoccupied with the loss and with the accompanying painful feelings.

Depression may follow. You are confused, angry, anxious, afraid, and so alone. You can no longer concentrate on your daily tasks, and you feel lost as life shifts into slow motion. You feel a piercing pain in your heart, a gnawing terror in your stomach. You are so absorbed by the loss that you can think of little else. You may cry and scream out in protest or sink into a corner of darkness and despair. Often you feel anger at God, others, yourself, or life in general. Often physical and psychological symptoms appear as body and soul express the pain of the heart. The most difficult thing in life is to accept its brokenness, its fragility, its temporariness, its changes, and its disappointments.

Unfulfilled Expectations and Broken Dreams

Some of the greatest disappointments in life come from unfulfilled expectations and broken dreams. Pain occurs when the realities of life clash with the ideal you feel you ought to be experiencing. Unrealized goals, shattered dreams, unfulfilled expectations, and relentless yearnings of the heart create pockets of deep pain. Loss occurs when life is different from what you wanted or expected. You grieve for that which you never had, for that which you no longer have, and for that which you will never have.

The Pain of Guilt

One of life's greatest pains is the feeling that you have failed and have not lived up to your own expectations or the expectations of others. You feel that you have disappointed yourself, others, and God. At such times, feelings of guilt and shame consume the soul. Everyone fails sometimes, and you may feel very badly about your failures. Those who experience major failures know the pain of deep embarrassment and shame. Perhaps the greatest tragedy that can befall you is to feel so badly about yourself that you engage in self-loathing and condemnation.

David expressed his guilt of a major moral failure in these grievous words:

> **My guilt has overwhelmed me**
> **like a burden too heavy to bear.**
> **My wounds fester and are loathsome**
> **because of my sinful folly.**
> **I am bowed down and brought very low;**
> **all day long I go about mourning.**
> **My back is filled with searing pain;**
> **there is no health in my body.**
> **I am feeble and utterly crushed;**
> **I groan in anguish of heart**.
> — Psalm 38:4-8

Spiritual Pain

Spiritual pain occurs when one feels abandoned by God during painful times. You may ask, "If God loves me and desires what is best for me, why does He allow pain and suffering in my life?" It is not uncommon to feel separated from God during these dark nights of the soul. You may feel that God doesn't care or that He is not in control of what happens to you. You may feel let down by God as you mourn the loss of your expectations about God's care and protection. Spiritual pain can lead to anger, anger to cynicism, and cynicism to apathy. Many persons have known the deep spiritual darkness that cries out, "My God, my God, why have you forsaken me?"

Pain Is Not Evil

You need to remind yourself, however, that pain is not evil. It is a natural response to the hurts, disappointments, and losses of life. You cannot help but be in pain if you have been hurt. Pain is a reality that you must learn to live with. Although you spend much time and effort trying to avoid pain, it happens nonetheless. It is what you do with pain that affects you for good or for ill.

Pain is a natural response to the hurts, disappointments, and losses of life.

Whatever it is, wherever it comes from, and whether it comes suddenly or gradually, this inner pain is very real. The gut wrenches and twists, a deep stabbing is felt in the heart, anxiety swirls around you like a devastating storm, you become "sick to your stomach" and feel that your heart is breaking. You feel that you cannot endure another moment of this tormenting pain. You feel that you are going to lose your mind. The pain can be so acute that you wish you could die so that you would no longer hurt this way. I know. I've been there. Pain is real. So very real.

CHAPTER 2

PAIN: THE GIFT NOBODY WANTS

Everyone experiences physical pain. It really hurts when you pinch your finger in a door, break a leg, recuperate from surgery, or just have a headache. You know where it hurts and you usually know why it hurts. Often there is physical evidence such as cuts, bruises, swelling, broken bones, bleeding, or an infection. No question about it. It hurts! Physicians frequently give medication to ease the pain.

Physical pain is essential for survival. It alerts you to the fact that something is wrong and needs attention. When you touch something that is too hot to handle, the scorching pain tells you to withdraw your hand immediately, before further damage occurs. The pain in your chest is a sign that you need medical attention. Your quick response could save your life.

In their book *Pain: The Gift Nobody Wants,* Dr. Paul Brand and Philip Yancey describe the ravages of the disease of leprosy (Hansen's disease) as the loss of pain sensation. Without the protection of pain, Dr. Brand discovered, leprosy patients were destroying themselves. They held hot items, walked on broken feet, cut themselves, exerted energy beyond their capacity, and suffered from infections, all without awareness of the injuries. Leprosy shuts down the pain sensors, numbing the pain cells of the extremities. Without the warning system of pain, destruction quickly follows. Physical pain is essential for survival.

It makes you pay attention to the injury. Proper care of the pain can lead to your healing. Dr. Brand exclaims: "Thank God for pain!"[1]

Emotional pain is a gift that calls you to pay attention to an injury that has occurred.

Emotional pain, like physical pain, is also a gift that nobody wants. It calls attention, however, to the fact that something significant is happening that needs your attention. The pain of loss tells you that you have suffered a severe injury. It is calling you to stop, look, feel, and listen—to pay attention to the injury.

The pain calls for help to deal with it. It's wise to reach out to others for help—a friend, a pastor, a therapist. Sharing the pain helps you to face it, to talk about it, to deal with it. It helps you to face the reality of the loss and the fact that the loss is painful. If the pain is not opened and released, if it is stuffed inside, it will begin to express itself in destructive ways, causing psychological and physical symptoms. Sharing your pain is like lancing it with a scalpel. It will hurt. But the time and effort of caring for your loss will begin the journey toward healing.

If you break your arm in a fall, you go to the emergency room of a hospital to be treated. You emerge with your arm in a sling. You take good care of your broken arm. You may also be treated by a physical therapist who will help you to regain mobility and strength.

How do you heal a broken heart? Very carefully. You seek the help you need to find healing. You open your life to the care of God and others. Tending to your emotional wounds will also lead to their healing.

PRINCIPLES

---

1. Pain is.

2. Emotional pain is not evil. It is a natural response to loss, disappointment, fear, guilt, or failure.

3. Emotional pain is a deep, inner aching of the soul.

4. Emotional pain must be released if you want to move toward healing.

5. Loss occurs when life is different from what you wanted or expected.

6. How you deal with your pain will affect you for good or for ill.

7. Emotional pain is a gift that calls you to pay attention to a significant loss that has occurred.

8. The time and effort of caring for your injury will begin to move you toward healing.

DEALING WITH PAIN

CHAPTER 3

RELEASING THE PAIN

"There is a time for everything:
a time to weep . . .
a time to mourn . . ."
— Ecclesiastes 3:1, 4

When you are hurting, you need help in expressing and releasing the pain. You may need some encouragement, some prompters to help release painful feelings. The sentence completions below will help you to identify and express your pain. Begin by acknowledging and expressing the pain to yourself, sharing it with a trusted friend, and offering it as a prayer to God.

"Right now I am feeling . . . "

"I'm hurting right now because . . . "

"The loss I am facing is . . . "

"I need help in dealing with . . . "

The Healing of Tears

T. DeWitt Talmage wrote, "Help me to explain a tear. A chemist will tell you that it is made of salt and lime and other component parts; but he misses the chief ingredients—the acid of a soured life, the viperine sting of a bitter memory, the fragments of a broken heart. I will tell you what a tear is: it is agony in solution."

Tom Lutz, in a study of crying, writes: "Weeping is a human universal. Throughout history, and in every culture, emotional tears are shed—everyone, everywhere, cries at some time. . . . And weeping is exclusively human. As far as we know, no other animal produces emotional tears."[2]

Crying can release deep, pent-up feelings and internal tensions. Sobbing deeply from the heart is a natural, healthy release of painful emotions. Tears are the language of the soul. They express the pain of the heart that words cannot express. Many people feel better after a good cry. Crying has a way of cleansing the soul. It provides a way to release pain. Sometimes screaming and pounding on a soft object will also help to release the pain. As the wise man has said, "There is a time to weep" (Ecclesiastes 3:4).

Tears are the language of the soul.

Only God can understand the real meaning of your tears. Only God knows what you are feeling inside. The psalmist describes the attention and tender heart of God when He sees your tears:

> **You have seen me tossing and turning
>   through the night.
> You have collected all my tears
>   and preserved them in your bottle!
> You have recorded every one
>   in your book.**
> — Psalm 56:8 (TLB)

The Relief of Releasing

I went into the emergency room of a local hospital one day to have my infected finger treated. It hurt when the physician cut the whole way around the fingernail without an anesthetic to release the infection. It came pouring out. For a moment I gasped in pain. My eyes filled with tears. As the doctor pulled out the razor-like knife, I said to him, "I don't swear, but if I call on God to help me, please understand." All I could say was "Oh, my God!" as he cut into the quick. And I meant it. I was calling out for help. It hurt!

Yes, life hurts at times, really hurts. And sometimes dealing with the pain intensifies the hurt for a time. It hurts to open the wound, to talk about the loss, to let yourself feel the pain, to squeeze out the infection. Some people choose not to face the pain. But the healing that comes in opening the wound is worth the pain you have to endure. The pain you turn from is the pain you run into. Embracing the pain, giving yourself permission to grieve, asking for help, and being patient with yourself as you walk through your pain will begin to create an atmosphere for healing. If you care for your wound, healing will come.

The pain you turn from is the pain you run into.

Reactions May Be Delayed

An individual I was counseling for depression told of her reaction following a stroke that had happened three months earlier. Her safe world had suddenly been shattered by a life-threatening event. When I asked her how she had dealt with that situation initially, she responded: "First I went into shock. Then I went onto automatic pilot. Now I am crashing. I'm crying a lot now and feeling very depressed. I'm starting to realize what happened to me. I could have died. I'm too young for that!"

The reality of her loss occurred some time after the fact. When initially faced with a serious threat, her body and emotions went into shock. She felt numb and dazed, unable to grasp the reality of what had happened. Shock was her body's and emotions' way of absorbing the loss, helping her to survive the initial jolt.

Then she went on automatic pilot. During this time she simply kept breathing and performing the essential routine of basic survival. She described feeling stunned, almost as if in a state of amnesia. Her life seemed to be going in slow motion. Initially, she was not able to comprehend what had happened and how it would affect her life, yet she knew that a serious loss had occurred. The body and emotions were helping her to survive the pain by leading her to face it one step at a time.

At a later time—it usually comes gradually—her feelings began to catch up with the loss. The reality of the loss began to affect her emotions more directly. Now she began the painful process of facing the loss of her security and the well-being that she had taken for granted. Gradually the painful reality of the loss began to come more clearly into focus. Her grieving now entered into a heightened stage. She was asking for help to deal with it.

Healing Is a Process

Recovering from the wounds of life is a process, not an event. It takes time, energy, honesty, and courage to grieve. There are no quick "fixes." Although grief is a universal experience, it is intensely personal. Everyone grieves in his or her own way, place, and time. There is no one right way to grieve. You need to grieve in your own special way, to hear your feelings, follow your heart, express your pain, and grieve your loss. The experience of grieving—a natural emotional response to loss—is nature's way of healing a broken heart. Embracing the pain and giving yourself permission to grieve are crucial for recovery. As Granger Westberg has written, " 'Grieve—not as those who have no hope', but please, when you have something worth grieving about, go ahead and grieve."[3]

**Grieving is nature's way of healing
a broken heart.**

Grieving Creates a Special Place for Memories

Some people are afraid to grieve because they see grieving as a letting go of their loved ones and moving on without them. They feel that if they grieve they are acknowledging their loss and leaving their loved ones behind. This is a common but incorrect view of grieving. Grieving does not mean that you mourn your losses and then move on without your loved ones. Oh, no! You want to remember your loved ones in ways that will bring encouragement and comfort to your heart. In fact, grieving is healthy and necessary because it creates a special place deep in your heart where your loved ones will always be. The process of grieving helps to place your loved ones at another place in your life.

Grieving involves reviewing your special relationships with your loved ones and embedding those special memories forever into your heart. Grieving creates a special place for your treasured and precious memories. It helps you to let go of the longed-for physical presence of your loved ones as you internalize their emotional and spiritual meaning. In preserving those memories, you are creating a special memorial to their lives that will always be with you and, in time, bring you comfort.

Grieving creates a special place in your heart for your treasured and precious memories.

Grief Lingers On

There is no easy or quick solution for dealing with emotional pain. Grieving is a painful, lingering, emotionally-consuming process. It takes time, energy, honesty, and courage to grieve. Efforts to understand the loss and move toward accepting it will increase your pain for the moment. Searching for ways of walking through the pain is itself a painful process. It is painful to turn and face your loss. Grieving is not something you do and then get over. Instead, you must experience your grief, move toward it and through it, follow its leading, and look for the resources that will help you make it.

Confusion comes when you think that your deepest pain occurred at the time of the loss or shortly thereafter. In cases of severe loss, this overwhelming sense of loss can occur anytime after the happening. Sometimes, for no particular known reason, waves of recurring grief can envelop you and bring you to the breaking point. The intensity of the grief may be even stronger at those times than it was initially, when you may have been in shock or denial. Anniversaries, birthdays, holidays, and other events and occasions that evoke memories of a loved one can exacerbate the feelings of grief.

The Strength To Go On

Pain comes to everyone. Life is filled with changes,

losses, suffering, and difficulties. It is natural to feel pain when you have suffered a loss. To be restored, you must face your losses, deal with them, get help if you need to, and take time to grieve. It's a slow and painful process, one you will tend to avoid and deny if you can. It hurts to face pain, to accept the permanency of a loss, to grieve your losses. You don't want to cut grief short. It takes time for grief to do its healing work. You are not ready to move on until you have grieved your losses.

As you mourn what was lost, work through the pain and express your feelings about it, eventually you will take up normal activities once again. When faith and hope return, you will find the strength to go on. As life goes on, the pain begins to lose its intensity and you move slowly and painfully back into the mainstream of life. Grieving then helps you to get to the place were you can focus on what yet remains. When you invest your life in what you still have, life takes on meaning again and you find the strength to go on.

When faith and hope return, you will find the strength to go on.

People are resilient. They do come back from deep shocks to live and laugh again. It is indeed a gift of God's grace that people come back from the most devastating experiences to find meaning and hope in life again. As the psalmist said, "Weeping may endure for the night, but joy comes in the morning" (Psalm 30:5, NKJV).

CHAPTER 4

LIVING WITH PAIN

Some painful situations are of a minor, temporary nature and the pain is short-lived. You find a solution, the situation dissolves, or you learn to live with it. You make adjustments and go on. You hurt while you are going through it, but time and grace heal the pain.

Other painful experiences come as traumatic losses, as in the sudden death of a loved one. You need a special kind of help to get through the shock and utter disbelief of such tragedy. You must walk through a funeral and deal with the aftershock of intense feelings of loss. You deal with such feelings as shock, denial, protest, anger, blame, and guilt. It is a terrible dark night that needs special help to get through.

Major losses that are of an ongoing nature in which the pain is very intense can also be experienced: a separation in a marriage, an unwanted divorce, estrangement from children, false accusations, guilt from an indiscretion or failure, the loss of a job, the loss of health and independence. In such losses, you cannot have a funeral or "good-bye" type of experience that begins to bring closure. Others may not understand the depth of your pain. So there may be no one to grieve with you. The reality of the pain is continuous. You go to sleep at night with the ache in your heart and it will be there when you wake in the morning. Life has placed you in a position where you are called to move ahead with an empty place in your heart, with a broken dream, as the heart aches daily. You are called to live with the pain.

Greg called me one day and asked to meet with me. He told me a sad story of how his wife of two years had moved out and had taken their little daughter with her. For weeks he wandered around in his own house in shock and disbelief. He became lost in his pain. He made many attempts to reconcile the marriage, but she refused to hear or believe that things would change. She had been hurt deeply in a prior relationship and she was not going to risk any more of herself.

At first, Greg was obsessed with his loss. He could not go to work nor follow his daily routine. He lay on the bed and cried and pounded the pillow. He refused to eat. He considered suicide. He became very angry, first with his wife, then with himself. He began to blame himself for what had happened and spent a lot of time berating himself. "If only, if only, if only . . ." he had done this or that to save the marriage. He cried again and again that he could not go on without her. He hurt too much.

Time went on and she did not return. I spent a lot of time listening to him and helping him to face and express the pain of his loss. The following conversation, after several months of counseling, revealed his struggle of living with the ongoing pain.

N: "Have you ever considered living with your pain?"

G: "What do you mean by that? 'Living with your pain'?"

N: "I know you are hurting a lot. You've experienced a terrible blow."

G: "No one would ever understand unless they've been through it."

N: "I understand. It's hard to move on when you're hurting so badly."

G: "Hard to move on? I can't move on! I'm stuck— right here in the middle of my gut. Right here!"

N: "I know it hurts. We've talked a lot about what happened and how it has affected you. What I'm suggesting is that sometimes we have to move on even though we are hurting."

G: "I don't know how to do that."

N: "I know it's very painful to move on when you're hurting so badly."

G: "How do I move on? I can't stop thinking of her. Everything I do and see reminds me of her. I can't let go. She's all I have."

N: "It's very hard to move on when you're hurting."

G: "You keep saying that."

N: "I know . . . I know."

G: "When you talk about letting go of my pain and moving on, I don't know what you mean."

N: "I'm not talking about letting go of your pain. I'm talking about learning to live with your pain, taking your pain with you as you go back to work, and gradually starting to live a more normal life."

G: "But that means giving up my hopes of my wife and daughter returning."

N: "Yes, it may feel that way to you. But what I'm suggesting is that you go back to work, get out with your friends, and start visiting your daughter. Just starting gradually to come back to life. It will be hard and painful to do this because it will move you into a new area of reality in which you will have to make adjustments to your loss, begin accepting what happened, and start to meet it with a different response."

G: "I don't want to do that. I want her to come back."

N: "I know you're grieving for her and want her to come back. The reality is that she's gone and says she is not coming back. That's the hard stuff for you to face. What I'm suggesting is that maybe you can learn to live with your pain and begin to look for ways to go on."

In our times together, we continued to talk about what it would be like to learn to live with the pain. How he could hurt and still go back to work. How he could hurt and still go out with his friends. How he could hurt and still believe in God, in himself, and in life. How he could hurt and still be a father to his daughter. How he could hurt and go on with his life, changed, for sure, but still go on.

**Pain forces you to move on as you look
for relief and comfort.**

Slowly he began to stir back to life. He came to view his pain not as an enemy that wanted to destroy him but as a natural result of his loss. He couldn't help but hurt. But now the pain was helping him to move on because he hurt too much to stay stuck at that spot. The pain forced him to look for ways to deal with his loss other than becoming immobilized by it. The pain forced him to look for relief and comfort.

In time, he was able to move on and return to a more normal routine. The more his life went on, the more his pain subsided. The more his pain subsided, the freer and happier he became. Eventually he was able to return to a near-normal life a much wiser and more mature man.

Life can hurt and still be worth living.

Slowly, painfully, he came to see that life can hurt and still be worth living. Gradually he discovered that there is life in the midst of pain. He came to see that there was more to life than the loss he had suffered. He discovered, to his surprise, that there is life after loss. He chose to go on.

As you mourn what you have lost, work through the pain and express your hurt, eventually you will take up normal activities once again. When faith and hope return, you will find the strength to go on. As life goes on, the pain begins to lose its intensity and you move slowly back into the mainstream of life. You may feel the pain of your loss for the rest of your life. Some losses ache daily. But you can learn to live with the pain and find a reason to go on.

There is life after loss.

CHAPTER 5

TAKING A BREAK

I remember a time when I was hurting badly. I was obsessing with a very personal issue and living off my fear. I was hurting as deeply as I had ever hurt. I was crumbling inside. Friends called and invited my wife and me out for dinner. I didn't want to go. I didn't feel like socializing, eating or having a good time. I felt too bad for all that good stuff. But I went, partly on my wife's insistence, and ended up relaxing and having a good time. I saw that life goes on in spite of my pain and that I can take a break from pain and enjoy life. It was a time of healing for me. Milton Erickson wrote: "Life will bring you pain all by itself. Your responsibility is to create joy."

You can take a break from pain and enjoy life.

It's okay to take a break from pain to become involved in other activities. If the mind and heart can take a rest, even for a moment, it helps the wounded spirit to heal. It's like taking some pressure off a broken leg by sitting down and elevating it for a moment. It's healing to take the pressure off your feelings and give them a rest, too.

So, in the midst of your pain, take a break. Do something else. Give yourself permission to relax. Friends can help you to schedule some joy in the midst of the painful times. The psalmist discovered that God prepared a table for him in the presence of his enemies. Remind yourself that you can deal with the pain later on. When you are aware that you will continue to grieve, you will be able to take a break from dwelling unremittingly on your grief.

If you have suffered a serious loss such as the death of a loved one, you will likely feel guilty the first times you go out and try to relax or do something pleasurable. How can I be enjoying myself, you ask, when one I love is no longer able to enjoy life? It doesn't feel right or seem fair. But you will discover, as others have, that moments of distraction from the pain become times of healing. You begin to discover, slowly and painfully, that there is life in the midst of pain and that life does go on. And, to your amazement, you will discover that life can be good again.

You discover that there is life in the midst of pain.

CHAPTER 6

LET FRIENDS HELP YOU

Caring and trustworthy friends can help you face and express pain. Friends can encourage you to be open and honest. Sharing your grief with someone who cares about you is very healing.

When you are deep in pain, you look for reasons for your suffering. It's so easy to blame yourself and to feel guilty for what is happening. "It must be something I did," you might tell yourself. "If bad things are happening to me, then I must be a bad person." You may feel that you are being punished by God for something you did. In those feelings of self-condemnation, you tend to isolate yourself from God and others. You feel that God and the world have turned against you. You pull down an emotional curtain and cover your head with blankets of self-pity and shame.

While you are grieving, you may wish to be left alone. This is a common feeling during grief. But too much loneliness will only add to the pain and the sense of isolation. You need to draw close to friends for companionship and comfort. At such times, friends enter into your life and give you opportunities to share your grief with them. To grieve in a healthy way you need others to talk with about your loss, to hold you, to feel your pain, to cry with you, to protest with you. You move toward healing when you share your inner pain with those who care about you.

I Chronicles 21 tells of the acute grief Ephraim experienced after two of his sons were killed in a skirmish. His lingering grief affected his marriage. After Ephraim's brothers came to comfort and console him, his grief was relieved and his marriage restored.

Friends help you to grieve by talking with you about your loss. Talking about your pain puts words to what you are feeling. Feelings need avenues of expression. Talking about them helps to get the pain out. Talking helps you to face the reality of your loss, to express how the pain is touching your life. It gives meaning to what is going on within you. Your friends can help you to put words to your feelings, thus bringing the pain to the surface so you can hear it, feel it, face it, and begin dealing with it. Someone once said, "Words carve out coherence from a blur of feelings."

To grieve in a healthy way, you need to talk with friends about your pain.

Talking about your feelings helps put the pieces together. You begin to recognize what is going on. In times of sorrow, you feel an urge to talk about what has happened. It's your way of trying to get used to what has happened. It helps you to face the reality of the loss. Friends can encourage you, challenge you, give you a diversion from dwelling on the pain, make you laugh and cry, and listen to you. Sometimes they will share their own pain with you, which helps you to realize that pain affects others, too. Then you won't feel so alone. Friends help you feel that it's okay to be human, to hurt, to cry, to protest, to be yourself. They can lend their hope and faith to you. When you are grieving a loss, find someone you trust who understands and accepts your feelings. Then open your heart and share your deepest thoughts and feelings.

What Do You Need?

Ask yourself these questions as you consider the resources that are available to help you deal with painful times.

What do I need most from family and friends right now?

Who do I need to be with to help me face this pain?

Who can best help me to express this pain?

What do I need from God right now?

What has helped me deal with pain before?

Practical Ways To Deal With Pain

It's important to find ways to comfort and strengthen yourself during painful times. There are things you can do that will help to bring you through the long, hard days and the dark, fearful nights.

The following suggestions are offered not as substitutes for the hard work of grief but, rather, as activities that will help you to cope with times of pain.

- teach yourself to relax

- listen to soothing music

- engage in physical activities and exercises

- organize your day by breaking it down into time frames in which to accomplish certain tasks

- learn to care for yourself by getting rest, eating nutritious food, treating yourself to a pleasant happening

- surround yourself with family and friends

- be in areas where you will be with others

- when the pain becomes acute, stop and perform some conscious slowdown activity such as deep breathing, calling a friend, or engaging in prayer, scripture reading and meditation

- reach out to help someone else who is hurting

- join a self-help group where others are dealing with similar situations

- be patient with yourself; it takes a lot of time and energy to do the work of grieving

- become as involved in your normal daily activities as you are able

- seek professional help if your pain immobilizes you, if your depression is debilitating, if you are having physical pain, or if you have indications of prolonged or unnatural grief

- if you have any questions or concerns about your reactions to grief, talk with your pastor, a grief counselor, or another professional who understands the nature of grief

CHAPTER 7

FAITH ENCOURAGES GRIEVING

Yes, you hurt when you face the losses of life. But you can also do something else—you can draw from the deepest resources of faith to sustain you. Faith in God offers a source of comfort and strength to deal with the hurts of life. Faith gives you the courage to face pain in the awareness that God is with you. Friends can bring comfort. Physicians can prescribe medication. Psychotherapists can help you to talk about your pain. Grief counselors can help you work through the losses. But there is also a spiritual part of you that can find comfort only in God.

Henri Nouwen wrote: "Our life is full of brokenness—broken relationships, broken promises, broken expectations. How can we live with that brokenness without becoming bitter and resentful except by returning again and again to God's faithful presence in our lives."

What you believe about God affects how you see and deal with life's pains. If there is no hope beyond death, no faith by which to view the experiences of life beyond your earthly view, you will get stuck in the painful here-and-now without hope. Faith in God enables you to see hope in the midst of pain. It places the events of life within the context of God's enduring love.

**Faith in God enables you to see hope
in the midst of pain.**

Faith in God will not answer questions about suffering or provide quick fixes. Nor does faith in God take away the need to grieve. Grief is not a denial of faith. Faith in God's enduring love helps you to begin the painful process of letting go of that which you long for by trusting that God will gather unto Himself that which you have to let go. Faith in God helps you to grieve as you release into His care that which you can no longer bear. Faith provides a rich context of hope in which to experience pain and express grief. It is a hope into which you must eventually commit all things, including your own life. The Apostle Paul wrote that we need "not grieve as others do who have no hope" (I Thessalonians 4:13, RSV).

Faith provides a rich context of hope in which to experience pain and express grief.

Tim Hansel, the author of a book entitled *You Gotta Keep Dancin',* writes of his experience of pain following a fall from a glacier. In a chapter "Peace Inside the Pain", he writes of the way faith expresses itself in painful times:

> But one of the ways that our faith expresses itself is by our ability to be still, to be present, and not to panic or lose perspective. God still does his best work in the most difficult of circumstances. The Spirit is more powerful than the will, more powerful than the flesh, more powerful than pain, more powerful than guilt, even more powerful than our weakness and our doubt.

> We can experience the living Christ here and now, and our difficult circumstances will be the very opportunity for our faith to grow.[4]

CHAPTER 8

TRUST THE CAPTAIN

There are times when you have done your best and the storm rages on. The problem is still there, the pain continues, and you see no relief ahead. You have faced the pain, you have prayed much, you have cried much, you have shared with friends, you have sought counseling, but you continue to hurt. You can't really say "good-bye" because there is no closure. When you wake up in the morning, the pain is still there. You start another day with a heavy heart. In those times, you need to turn things over to the Captain of your soul.

One day my family and I were out on the Chincoteague Bay in Maryland, clamming and crabbing with friends. One of those swift and vicious storms blew up from the ocean without warning. Six small children and four adults were on the boat. Fortunately our captain had grown up on the bay and knew what action to take. He made us all lie down in the boat and covered us with blankets. Then he stood at the helm and turned the boat into the fury of the storm as he headed for shore.

The boat rocked wildly. The motor roared as the propeller was lifted up out of the water by each powerful wave. A few times I lifted my blanket to see what was happening. It was one of the most frightening experiences of my life. Angry, black clouds rolled overhead, lightning flashed in violent, white streaks, and the wind blew furiously. I could see no land. It was dark and scary. I prayed for the safety of my family as I pulled the blanket tightly around me. I'll never forget that time.

But I'll always remember a hopeful sight. My friend, the captain, stood tall and confident at the helm. He held the throttle steady. He looked straight ahead. He would occasionally reach for a towel to wipe the salt water out of his eyes. He could not see the distant shore, but he knew where he wanted to go. He remained steady, calm, and on course. We finally arrived, shaken up but safe.

After we packed up and were on the way to the captain's house for dinner, I asked him if he had been afraid we might not make it through the storm. "It was an awesome storm," he replied. "One of the worst I've ever seen. But I was not afraid. I grew up on this bay.

"My father and I built this boat," he continued. "We've been together in many storms. We built this boat to survive the storms. He taught me how to navigate through the storms. I had confidence that we would make it. After all, remember that I was in the boat with you."

In the dark and scary times, remember that the Captain of your soul is in the boat with you.

I learned something important from my captain friend that I often reflect upon when caught in one of the storms of life. There are some awesome moments when you have to stand tall and true and turn to face the fury of the storm. There is no way out but through it. You have to trust the Captain at the helm, endure the beating, manage the scary feelings, remain as calm as you can, pray for protection, and hold on. You cannot jump overboard, for you would surely drown. You must stay with the Captain, for He has been through these storms and knows what to do. You give the helm to the One who made the ship and knows the way through the storms. Wipe the tears from your eyes, ask the Captain Himself for faith to hold on, and wait for relief. Some storms rage out of control.. You are powerless to change what is happening. There is little else you can do but place the journey into the hands of your Captain, the Lord Jesus Christ, as you hold on to Him. Remember, He is in the boat with you.

> Jesus, Savior, pilot me
> Over life's tempestuous sea;
> Unknown waves before me roll,
> Hiding rocks and treacherous shoal.
> Chart and compass come from Thee;
> Jesus, Savior, pilot me.
>   — Edward Hopper

PRINCIPLES

1. Grieving helps you to face the reality of the loss and release the painful feelings.

2. When you are hurting, you may need help to express and release the pain.

3. It's healthy to cry. Tears are the language of the soul.

4. Grieving is nature's way of healing a broken heart.

5. The pain you run from is the pain you run into.

6. Recovering from the wounds of life is a process, not an event. Grieving is something that you experience, not overcome.

7. When faith and hope return, you will find the strength to go on.

8. Life can hurt and still be worth living.

9. There is life after loss.

10. Caring friends can help you to grieve.

11. Faith in God helps you to grieve as you entrust to Him that which you cannot have.

12. Faith is trusting the Captain of your soul to guide you through the storms and bring you safely home.

BIBLICAL PERSONALITIES AND PAIN

CHAPTER 9

DAVID

The Bible allows us to look into the hearts of God's people. It describes their successes and failures, their defeats and victories, their joys and sorrows. Their stories are painfully honest, yet always brimming with hope. Their disclosures help us to become honest with ourselves. Often people of faith are hesitant to share their struggles in the fear that they will appear to be weak. They believe they must always be strong in the face of adversity. But we can learn from the biblical characters of David and Jonathan, Elijah, Job, and the Apostles Paul and John. Their stories encourage us to be open about our pains and struggles.

David and Jonathan

David, the future king of Israel, developed a close relationship with King Saul's son, Jonathan. When these young men realized that their friendship would not survive Saul's madness, they met in a field to say goodbye. They wept together. Jonathan loved David "as he loved himself." Samuel reports that "David wept the most," which indicates the depth of his sorrow and his freedom to express it (I Samuel 20).

David and Jonathan faced their pain. They met to express their feelings, their grief, their sadness. They helped each other to deal with their feelings by facing their pain and sharing it openly with one another. They talked about it and wept together. That's always the healthiest way to deal with pain.

David's Loss at Ziklag

David knew another time of grief when he returned to his hometown, Ziklag, after a military adventure. He and his soldiers came home anticipating a happy reunion with their families. Instead, they found their city lying in ashes. The Amalekites had destroyed it and had taken captive all the women and children. Overlooking the place where their homes once stood, ". . . David and the people who were with him lifted up their voices and wept, until they had no more power to weep" (I Samuel 30:4, NKJV). These were strong, tough soldiers who faced death daily. But this day their feelings were tender. It was their loss. It was a time of personal and communal grief. They wept until they were exhausted, spent. Can you feel the intensity of their pain?

Then, overcome with grief, David's own soldiers began to plot his assassination. Usually grief looks to blame, to find someone responsible for the tragedy. Anger and blame are early expressions of grief. The story says that "each one was bitter in spirit because of his sons and daughters."

David strengthened himself in the Lord his God.

How would David respond to these threats to his life? "But David strengthened himself in the Lord his God" (I Samuel 30:6). The story doesn't tell how he strengthened himself, but I imagine it would have involved some or all of the following aspects.

First, I believe he remembered his anointing by the prophet Samuel to be king of Israel. David was just a lad when it happened, but he surely remembered that moment. David drew strength by remembering the promises of God. He believed that God would fulfill His word. The New

Testament says it like this: ". . . being confident of this, that he who began a good work in you will carry it on to completion until the day of Christ Jesus" (Philippians 1:6).

Second, he must have remembered that momentous occasion when he slew Goliath. God was with him when he faced his most noted enemy. David chose to face the heavily-armored Goliath in his homespun linen garment with just five smooth stones and a slingshot. As he faced Goliath, he said to him, "All those gathered here will know that it is not by sword or spear that the Lord saves; for the battle is the Lord's, and he will give all of you into our hands" (I Samuel 17:47). When David's own soldiers were about to kill him, he must have remembered that it was the Lord who delivered Goliath to him. The battle was not his own, but the Lord's.

Third, David recalled the faithfulness of God. By this time in his life, he could look back upon the many times God had been faithful. He had given Goliath into his hands. He had protected him from mad Saul many times. He had led him through many victorious battles. David believed that God had not brought him this far to leave him. He would not lift him up to let him down. David had learned to trust in the faithfulness of God.

**David had learned to trust in
the faithfulness of God.**

Fourth, David was a man of prayer. Following his narrow escape from threats to his own life at Ziklag, he sought the Lord in prayer about his future actions. Should he pursue the enemy or not? The Lord instructed David to pursue the enemy. As a result, David was victorious and rescued all the families that had been taken captive. When David sought the Lord, God's faithfulness prevailed once again.

The Loss of His Son

David experienced a time of intense grief at the death of his infant son who had been conceived in his sin of adultery with Bathsheba. The prophet Nathan warned David that the son born to Uriah's wife would die. When the child was stricken, David pleaded with God for the life of the child. He fasted and spent the nights in his house lying on the ground. His servants stood beside him and tried to get him to eat, but he refused to be comforted.

When his child died, his servants were afraid to tell him. "If he grieves this much now," they reasoned, "what will he do when he hears that the child has died?" But David, sensing that something had happened, asked if the child had died. When he heard the dreaded response, he did an unexpected thing. He got up from the ground, washed, changed his clothes, and went to the temple to worship God. Then he returned home and requested food. David's servants asked him why he had fasted and wept while the child was alive but, now that the child had died, got up and ate. David replied that while the child was still alive he had hoped that the Lord would be gracious and let the child live. "But now that he is dead, why should I fast? Can I bring him back again? I will go to him, but he will not return to me" (2 Samuel 12:22, 23).

In this story, two important aspects of David's grief emerge. First, his grief and mourning were complicated by guilt. The child had been born as a result of David's sin. The prophet Nathan had told him of God's displeasure and the tragedy that would befall him. The biblical account says that "the Lord struck the child that Uriah's wife had borne to David, and he became ill" (2 Samuel 12:15). David knew what was happening, and he knew why it was happening. He was experiencing compound grief. There was the grief of losing a son and there was his self-blame for his sin. He had brought suffering upon himself, his child, Bathsheba and Uriah. No one could comfort him during those pitiful times of remorse. His heart was broken to the core. David repented of his sin and cried out to God for mercy. He recognized that he had sinned and had done this evil in God's sight. Some of the penitent psalms were likely written by David at this time.

Second, David experienced something we know today as "anticipatory grief." As a lingering death is approaching, individuals will begin to grieve in anticipation of the death. Letting go, saying good-byes, and experiencing some of the anger, guilt, and blame are already beginning to happen. Thus, at the time of death, there can be a sense of relief. The struggle is over. The suffering is done. Much of the grief has already been acknowledged and expressed. Death in its finality brings new dimensions to grief, but the survivors are likely to move more quickly toward a normal lifestyle. David had grieved his loss. He was now ready to move on. He got up, washed himself, and went to the temple to worship God. If your grief takes you to the temple to worship God, you have placed your hope in the One who comforts you in all your sorrows.

CHAPTER 10

ELIJAH

Elijah was one of the most influential prophets of the Old Testament. As one of Israel's most dynamic religious leaders, he helped to shape the history of his day and dominated Hebrew thought for centuries to come.

In one of his most dramatic moments, he challenged the prophets of Baal to a showdown on Mount Carmel. Whose God was real? Elijah's God, the God of Israel, or Baal, the god of the Canaanites? Whose God would answer the prayers of His prophets to discharge fire from heaven to consume an offering each had prepared? The prophets of Baal prayed all day, but nothing happened. Elijah prayed to the God of Israel who answered his prayer with a dramatic display of fire and power. Elijah then slew the prophets of Baal to finish off the victory.

What a spectacular victory for Elijah! But the very next day Elijah found himself running for his life. Jezebel, the wife of King Ahab of Israel and a champion of Baal worship who led Israel into the gross immoralities of this popular religion, threatened to have Elijah killed within twenty-four hours. Elijah heard this news and ran for his life. He ran to Beersheba in Judah. There he left his servant behind and traveled yet another day into the desert. Tired and exhausted, he sat under a juniper tree and prayed that he might die. "I have had enough, Lord. Take my life; I am no better than my ancestors" (I Kings 19:4). Then he laid down under the juniper tree and fell asleep.

As he slept, an angel came and touched him. The angel told Elijah to get up and eat. A cake of bread and a jar of water had been prepared for him. Elijah ate and drank and then laid down again. The angel touched him the second time and told him to get up and eat. After he ate he was strengthened and traveled forty days and nights until he reached Horeb, the mountain of God.

At Horeb he entered into a cave, still depressed. His dialogue with God reveals more of his feelings. He felt alone and abandoned by God. He had been very zealous for the Lord. He had put his life on the line for Him. He felt that he was the only faithful prophet left in all of Israel, and now his enemies were trying to kill him.

Elijah's story offers insights on depression and how God deals with depression. Elijah was exhausted after his successful ministry on Mount Carmel. He did not have time to replenish his spirit. Many defeats come after great victories. The enemy knows when to attack. In his weariness, Elijah ran from the threats of Jezebel. He was so exhausted and depressed that he lay under a tree to die. Some of the symptoms of depression are loss of appetite, tiredness, sleepiness, and thoughts of dying. God came to his side in the ministry of an angel. The angel touched him, awakened him, and nourished him. Sometimes it takes the caring touch of God to rouse us from our fears and depressions.

Many defeats come after great victories.

Elijah then traveled on to the mountain of God. He turned his face toward God in the midst of his depression. He was still discouraged when he arrived at Horeb, and he spent the night in a cave. There he indulged in self-pity and complaints. He told God that he was the only prophet left in all of Israel who had not bowed his knee to Baal. But God did not leave him there alone. He called him forth and asked him what he was doing in the cave. After Elijah poured out his heart, God spoke to him in a gentle whisper. Elijah presented his complaints again. To deal with depression, we need to present our laments to God. He hears and understands. A person who is depressed needs someone to talk to and needs to hear a "gentle whisper" of encouragement.

God then responded in an unexpected way. He did not tell Elijah that he should not be feeling that way. He did not chide him for not trusting Him. He did not call attention to his self-pity or tell him to "snap out of it." No, He gave him an important assignment. He sent him on a mission. To accomplish the mission, Elijah had to go back the way he came. He had to face the fear that drove him into the cave. He had to go back and face that which he had been running from. Elijah learned that the best way to deal with depression was to turn and face it, walk back through the pain, and allow God to fulfill His purpose in his life.

**The best way to deal with depression is
to turn and face it.**

By giving him a special assignment, God expressed His confidence in Elijah. His life was not over. His mission was yet to be fulfilled. There was more of God's work to do. People who are depressed feel unworthy and inadequate. They feel that God can't use them anymore, not after this defeat, this sin, this problem, this pain, this grief, even this guilt. God wants strong and victorious men and women, they think. Successful, self-confident, energized, filled with power and charisma. The Spirit of God flowing through them in mighty power. Anointed. Surely God would not awaken them from a depression-induced sleep or call them from a cave of self-pity and send them forth to anoint kings and prophets. Surely not!

Yet you can never predict God. What you discard, He raises up. When you hide, He finds you. When you run from your fears, He helps you face them. When you give up, He sends an angel to revive you. When you are weak, He strengthens you. When you lie down depressed and alone, He raises you up and feeds you. When you feel inadequate, He sends you on another mission. He just won't let you lie there alone, afraid, depressed, and defeated. A divine assignment is an effective anti-depressant. So is the touch of an angel!

CHAPTER 11

JOB

Once there was a very righteous man named Job. He worked hard, sacrificed to God, prayed for his family, and helped the poor. He was a community leader, a successful businessman who had become wealthy. A better man than Job could not be found. The Lord described Job as a perfect and upright man who feared God and shunned evil.

One day it was all taken from him. His business collapsed, his servants were murdered, his children were killed, his cattle were stolen. Suddenly he became a broken and lonely man. Then he himself became ill and nearly died. He broke out in loathsome sores from head to foot. He sat among the ashes and scraped himself with a potsherd. His wife became bitter toward God. She said to Job, "Are you still holding on to your integrity? Curse God and die" (Job 2:9). In my own words: "Stand up to God and tell Him what you really think. Don't take it from Him. Defy Him to His face. Then die."

Job, the Old Testament epitome of tragedy, described his pain in very vivid terms:

> **Why did I not perish at birth,**
> **and die as I came from the womb?**
> **Why were there knees to receive me**
> **and breasts that I might be nursed?**
> **For now I would be lying down in peace;**
> **I would be asleep and at rest.**
>
> — Job 3:11-13

> **Even today my complaint is bitter;**
> **his hand is heavy in spite**
> **of my groaning.**
> **If only I knew where to find him;**
> **if only I could go to his dwelling!**
> — Job 23:1, 2

Job's three friends came to comfort him. When they saw that his grief was very great, they sat down on the ground and were silent for seven days and seven nights. They should have remained silent, but there is this strong need to explain suffering and to try to fix it. So, one by one, they began to speak. In long-winded speeches, each one tried to explain to Job the reason for his great suffering. All three concluded that he must have sinned against God. What else would explain these dramatic losses? Job was stunned by the stinging criticism of his friends. He asked them when their long-winded speeches would end. A despairing man, he said, should at least have the devotion of his friends (Job 6:14). He called them "miserable comforters" (Job 16:2).

Job complained bitterly to the Lord about his suffering. He questioned and challenged God. He accused God of not caring about him and not answering him. He complained to God that He was more gracious to the heathen than to His own children. At one point Job cried out, "God assails me and tears me in his anger and gnashes his teeth at me; my opponent fastens on me his piercing eyes" (Job 16:9). Again and again he expressed his longing to die. He felt that God had forsaken him. If only I knew where to find God, he cried, I could go to His throne and present my case to Him. "If only there were someone to arbitrate between us" (Job 9:33).

Then God confronted Job. He gave him a nature tour and allowed him to see the wonders and majesty of His creation. He then asked a series of questions about His creation that left Job writhing in humility. After Job saw a vision of God's greatness, he bowed before Him in deep contrition: "I am unworthy—how can I reply to you? I put my hand over my mouth. I spoke once, but I have no answer—twice, but I will say no more" (Job 40:4, 5). When God spoke again of His great creative powers, Job surrendered his protest: "Surely I spoke of things I did not understand, things too wonderful for me to know" (Job 42:3).

A vision of God's greatness will bring you to your knees.

Job emerged from his grief after God revealed His power and glory to him. Job had been focusing on his pain and losses, trying desperately to understand why all these things were happening to him.

When Job looked up from his pain to see God, he repented. He said to God, "My ears had heard of you but now my eyes have seen you. Therefore I despise myself and repent in dust and ashes" (Job 42:5, 6). To see God in His greatness and majesty lifted Job from his depression. Job finally discovered the real Comforter. It was God Himself! The God of majesty and power. The God of creation. The awesome, holy God! This was Job's God. It is interesting that God never answered Job's questions about why all this had happened to him. Instead, God revealed Himself! The healing of Job came when he saw the wonder and majesty of God and humbled himself at His feet. No more demands for explanations. No more protests. No more challenges. Job was awe-struck from seeing God. Silent. Repentant. Through this experience, Job learned that God was not the source of his pain. Rather, God was the source of his strength and comfort.

God is the source of your strength and comfort.

In spite of his pain and suffering, Job did not shut God out of his life. Even in his questions and protests, He never lost contact with God or gave up on Him. In his book *Disappointment with God*, Philip Yancey writes that it's better to contend with God than to shut Him out:

> One bold message in the Book of Job is that you can say anything to God. Throw at him your grief, your anger, your doubt, your bitterness, your betrayal, your disappointment—he can absorb them all. As often as not, spiritual giants of the Bible are shown *contending* with God. They prefer to go away limping, like Jacob, rather than to shut God out.[5]

Even though Job felt forsaken by God, he never lost hope. He held on. He was bashed and bruised, but he held on to his belief in a loving God even though his suffering of the moment could not support it. He didn't change his beliefs about God to fit into his experiences, even though he must have been tempted to change his whole view of a caring God. Rather, he held on to what he believed about God in the face of everything that challenged those beliefs.

**"Don't forget in the dark what
you learned in the light."**

Some of the greatest biblical statements of faith come from Job in the midst of his awesome suffering. These statements shine forth as lights in the darkness, as anchors of the soul, as reminders for you and me to respond to suffering out of our own faith. As someone wrote: "Don't forget in the dark what you learned in the light."

Though he slay me, yet will I hope in him; (13:15)

All the days of my hard service I will wait for my renewal to come. (14:14)

I know that my Redeemer lives, and that in the end he will stand upon the earth. And after my skin has been destroyed, yet in my flesh I will see God. (19:25, 26)

But he knows the way that I take; when he has tested me, I will come forth as gold. (23:10)

What you say to yourself when you are suffering is critical to the survival of your soul. In the midst of loss and suffering, you can affirm your faith in God and in His promises. Yes, you express your protests, your questions, and the grief that you feel. You must face and release those feelings. But your faith needs to be expressed, too. Much courage and hope come from affirming your faith in God during the hard times. "Even if I die in the midst of this struggle, I will still place my faith and hope in God! God is my refuge and strength! With His help, I will get through this struggle. God is with me. When it's all said and done, no matter what happens, God is still my God and I am His child. Nothing can separate me from His love. I will place my hope in Him."

CHAPTER 12

THE APOSTLE PAUL

The Apostle Paul was the most dynamic and influential evangelist of early Christianity. Following his dramatic conversion experience, he became the leading spokesperson for the Gospel of Christ. He traveled widely and established churches throughout Asia Minor. His letters to those growing and struggling churches form the basis for much of New Testament theology. Paul is regarded as the greatest shaper of Christian thought.

Paul's Experiences of Suffering

The great Apostle suffered much from natural disasters, a personal problem he called a "thorn in the flesh," and persecution. In the end, he experienced martyrdom. Paul's life reveals some helpful truths regarding suffering.

We often wonder why God answers prayers for deliverance and protection in some situations and not in others. At one point God delivered Daniel from the lions' den. An angel came and closed the lions' mouths. In other situations, thousands of believers were fed to the lions for entertainment in the great Roman coliseum. Many of these early, brave Christians prayed for deliverance. Daniel was one of their heroes. But no angel came to shut the lions' mouths those times. One by one the Christians were torn to shreds before cheering crowds.

Jail Scene 1:

The Apostle Paul knew some miraculous deliverances

and some experiences that appeared to be defeats. In one situation, he and Silas were stripped, beaten, and thrown into prison for casting an evil spirit out of a fortuneteller. They were placed in the inner cell of the jail with their feet in stocks. At midnight, as they were praying and singing hymns, there was a violent earthquake that opened the prison doors and loosed everyone's chains. The jailer, thinking everyone had escaped, was about to kill himself when Paul stopped him by shouting that everyone was there. The jailer fell trembling before Paul and Silas and asked what he had to do to be saved. That's when Paul spoke those well-known words: "Believe in the Lord Jesus, and you will be saved—you and your household." After Paul and Silas ministered to him and to all the others in the house, the jailer and his family were baptized. The jailer was filled with joy because he had come to believe in God (Acts 16).

**Praising God in the midnight of your
life will set you free from fear.**

The Apostle Paul surely rejoiced in that mighty display of God's saving power. God had just delivered him in such a miraculous way. Paul certainly knew that God was with him and watching over him. Even the jailer heard the Gospel and was saved! What a great victory for a great man of God!

Jail Scene 2:

But another jail scene happened many years later in Rome. Paul was again in jail for preaching the Gospel. This time he was under house arrest, chained to a guard. This time there were no earthquakes, no angels sent to deliver him. While in prison, Paul wrote to his fellow Christians about suffering for Christ, running the race, crossing the finish line, and being faithful to the end.

**Rich treasures of faith can come forth
from the hard times of your life.**

There was no deliverance from prison this time. He was about to die for his faith. Yet he was still praising God in this midnight of his life. He was preaching and teaching the Gospel every opportunity he had. Many of his precious letters to the saints came from the days he spent in jail. What rich treasures of the faith came forth from the hard times of this great apostle's life.

In some situations God rescues you from suffering and sets you free. At other times God's grace is sufficient for your needs. He does not always rescue you from harm and danger. In each situation of Paul's suffering, God responded in a different way with His care, depending upon His will for Paul's life. There were times God took Paul through his struggles; there were other times He took him out. When God did not rescue Paul, He provided grace sufficient for his need. At all times the keeping power of God was evident. Paul allowed God to direct him through his trials. Thus he could write that in all things God works for the good of those who love Him.

**It is a great miracle to be rescued,
but it is a divine thing to be kept.**

At some points in your faith journey, God is more interested in keeping you than in rescuing you. When you struggle, you cry out to God to be rescued from harm and danger, from your pain and grief. It is a great miracle to be rescued, but it is a divine thing to be kept. As Tim Hansel wrote in his journal: "God will never lead you where his grace cannot keep you."[6]

CHAPTER 13

THE APOSTLE JOHN

The Apostle John, the "beloved" disciple of Jesus, experienced grief that is common to life. Toward the end of his life, he was banished to the island of Patmos because of his testimony for Jesus Christ. Patmos was the scene of his visions recorded in Revelation which describe both the great and final cosmic struggle between Jesus and Satan and the triumph of Christ and His Church.

In one of his visions, John saw a scroll in the right hand of Jesus the Lamb. The scroll contained the revelation of God. An angel asked, "Who is worthy to break the seals and open the scroll?" But no one could be found in heaven or on the earth or under the earth who could open the scroll.

"I wept and wept," John wrote, until "one of the elders said to me, 'Do not weep! See, the Lion of the tribe of Judah, the Root of David, has triumphed'" (Revelation 5:4, 5).

There is weeping that comes from a grieving heart when the truths of God cannot be made known to those who need their saving message. A pastor's heart is broken because a person he cares about does not respond to the truth of God's Word. A husband is brokenhearted because his wife will not open the Word of Life. A mother weeps for her son who says he no longer believes in God. A father cries for a daughter who has run away from home and joined a cult. Many tears have been shed by those who care about loved ones who have chosen to live in spiritual darkness, who cannot or who refuse to open the scroll.

Jeremiah the prophet stated that his eyes would weep bitterly, overflowing with tears because the people of Israel would be taken captive (Jeremiah 13:17). He wept for Israel's spiritual captivity before he wept for their political captivity. "Oh, that my eyes were a fountain of tears; I would weep forever; I would sob day and night for the slain of my people" (9:1, TLB).

The prophet Nehemiah sat down and wept when he heard of the deplorable conditions of the Jewish remnant who survived the exile. The wall of Jerusalem had been broken down, and the gates of the city had been burned with fire. Nehemiah wept, mourned, fasted, and prayed. These terrible conditions had all come about because his people had forsaken the Lord their God.

Jesus wept when He looked out over Jerusalem and saw its spiritual blindness:

> **As he approached Jerusalem and saw the city, he wept over it and said, "If you, even you, had only known on this day what would bring you peace—but now it is hidden from your eyes. . . . you do not recognize the time of God's coming to you."**
> -- Luke 19:41, 42, 44

Some of the deepest pains in life are caused by loved ones' spiritual blindness. They do not recognize the time of Christ's coming. They have chosen to live without God. Their lives are often in shambles as they move from thing to thing or person to person, always looking for that one experience that will satisfy the deep thirst of the soul to know God. They have no awareness of the evil they court, the lives they are affecting, the pain they are bringing to others, and the messes they leave behind. The spiritual hardening of the heart is cause for weeping.

Summary

Biblical personalities knew the ecstasy of victory and the agony of defeat. They knew and loved God, but they also knew the pains, sins, and griefs of life. It is helpful to see the brokenness of their hearts and the openness of their faith. These heroes of faith are presented in both their divinity and their humanity so that you might become more familiar with your divinity and your humanity. They brought some of their griefs upon themselves. Others were brought upon them by evil people and forces. And, in some cases, God inflicted painful events to correct the paths of His wayward children.

You can feel a oneness with the heroes of your faith. They hurt and cried, too. They struggled in trying to love and serve a God whose ways they did not often understand and at times protested. Yet they faced and expressed their pain in the belief that God would hear their cries. Even God the Creator is described as One who is grieved and whose heart is filled with pain (Genesis 6:6). Thus, as a person of faith, you, too, can allow yourself to feel pain, to express it, and to cry out to God for help.

The question is not so much "Why is this happening to me?" as it is "God, how can I draw close to You to find your strength and comfort?" You will never fully understand who God is, what He is up to, and how He uses the events of your life to fit into His plans. Your response to God must be one of faith that trusts Him with both the process and the outcome of your life. Faith is trusting in

God when you don't understand His way in your life. Your response to what is happening will shape you for the plans God has for you.

Faith is trusting in God when you don't understand His way in your life.

The heroes of faith teach that life is filled with struggle and rest, strife and peace, defeats and victories, laments and praises. You cannot separate the good and the bad and take only what fits into your theology. No, life comes to you every day as it is. Somehow, by God's grace, you deal with the mixture of good and evil in the faith that God can use those experiences to make Himself known, to forge your faith, and to accomplish His purpose in your life. It is your response to God's working in your life that shapes your faith. Like the heroes of faith, you believe that He loves you and that He is with you in the midst of your struggles. You continue to seek Him in the midst of your pain and confusion. You need not be afraid to question His ways or to protest His doings, but you keep coming to Him. You keep following Him. You keep hoping in Him. You journey on in faith, day by day, trusting in the faithfulness of God to keep you. Your faith does not rest in your understanding; it rests in your believing. It's a faith that says, "Even though I don't understand Your ways, O God, yet will I trust You. Grant me the faith to yield to You. I am Your child. You are my God!"

Faith does not rest in understanding; it rests in believing.

PRINCIPLES

---

1. **The Bible allows you to look into the hearts of God's people.**

2. **Like David, you can strengthen yourself in the Lord your God in times of trouble.**

3. **The best way to deal with depression is to turn and face it.**

4. **God Himself is the source of your strength and comfort.**

5. **"Don't forget in the dark what you learned in the light."**

6. **Great courage and hope come from affirming your faith in God in the hard times.**

7. **Praising God in the midnight of your life can set you free from fear.**

8. **Faith is trusting in God when you don't understand His way in your life.**

9. **Rich treasures of faith can be found in the hard places.**

10. **"God will never lead you where His grace cannot keep you."**

11. **Your response to God's working in your life shapes your faith.**

12. **Faith does not rest in understanding; it rests in believing.**

- - - - - - - - - - - - - SECTION 4 - - - - - - - - - - - - - -

RESPONSES TO PAIN

When I was in distress, I sought the Lord.
— Psalm 77:2

CHAPTER 14

A NEGATIVE RESPONSE TO PAIN

When you are hit with a painful experience, you try to understand what is happening and why it is happening. Your mind scans all possible causes. Is it something I did? Is God doing this to me? Is God angry with me? Or is the evil one trying to knock me down? Am I being tested like Job?

Your response to emotional pain can lead to despair or to growth. You can bemoan your lot, curse the darkness, turn away from God, and become hostile and cynical. Or you can allow pain to draw you closer to God, look for the good to come forth, and trust that God will provide a way through.

In your reaction to pain, you will experience many different responses. You search for the responses that will help you get through the hard times. No one can see only the good side of pain. Sometimes a response to pain raises questions about the goodness of God. My concern is not so much the questions, the doubts, or the range of responses as it is the overall direction in which you are moving. Ultimately, what will this pain accomplish in your life?

First, consider some negative reactions to pain.

1. God Is Punishing Me

During a time of suffering, you may feel that you are being punished for a real or an imaginary indiscretion. In effect, this position says, "If I feel this bad, then I must be bad." The pain is seen as a result of God's action. And, of course, you, like all of us, can find many times when you failed God and others, when you sinned.

The Teachings of Jesus

Jesus addressed the issue of innocence and guilt in two separate incidents in which people were killed. In the case of the Galileans who were killed by Pilate as they prepared their sacrifices, Jesus asked if those who were killed were worse sinners than all the other Galileans. He answered His own question forthrightly: "I tell you, no!" (Luke 13:3).

In another tragedy, a tower fell in Siloam and killed eighteen people. Jesus asked if the victims were worse offenders than all the others who lived in Jerusalem. Again He replied very clearly: "I tell you, no!" (Luke 13:5). Jesus also said that the Father "causes his sun to rise on the evil and on the good, and sends rain on the righteous and the unrighteous" (Matthew 5:4). In this teaching, Jesus talks about the universality of sin and makes clear the need of everyone for repentance.

Jesus taught that it rains on the righteous and on the unrighteous.

One day Jesus healed a man who was blind from birth. The disciples wanted to know who had sinned, this man or his parents, that he had been born blind. Jesus replied that neither the man nor his parents had sinned but that he had been born blind that the work of God might be displayed in his life (John 9:1-3).

It is simply not true that if you live a righteous life you will be free from life's tragedies and pains. Certainly there are some griefs you bring upon yourself that come from poor attitudes, wrong decisions, harmful habits, lack of godly knowledge, or an immoral lifestyle. But even if you live an upright life, you are not exempt from the imperfections, trials, problems, pains, or injustices of life. The righteous will also experience the difficulties, injustices, and griefs of life. Pain is not punishment. Pain comes to everyone.

**Living a good life will not free you
from the pains of life.**

---

2. If God Loves Me, He Will Keep Me from Pain

In this position, God is equated with pleasure and peace, with the good things of life. "If He loves me, He will spare me from troubles and calamities. He will take care of me and keep me from pain." I once heard a person say, "If there is a God, I would not be hurting this badly."

Why Is This Happening to Me?

"God, if You love me, why is this happening to me?" This is a familiar cry in Scripture. One of Israel's great warriors, Gideon, felt the pain of Israel's seven years of captivity to their enemy the Midianites. When an angel visited him and said, "The Lord is with you, mighty warrior," Gideon didn't stop to say, "Thank you, sir. I needed that!" Instead he protested: "But sir, if the Lord is with us, why has all this happened to us?" (Judges 6:13). This is a common response to pain. If the Lord loves you, if He is with you, why has all this happened to you?

You hear this familiar cry again when Jesus approaches Martha at the death of her brother, Lazarus. Her first response is a protest: "If you had been here, my brother would not have died" (John 11:21). You know, "Where were You when I needed You?" And, of course, the question of Christ from the cross often expresses the agony of those in the loneliness of pain: "My God, my God, why have you forsaken me?" (Matthew 27:46).

Children of God look for the intervention of God to shield them from evil. Children from Christian homes learned many Bible stories about how God protected and delivered His people from their ememies. There was Daniel saved in the lions' den, the three Hebrew children protected in the fiery furnace, the Red Sea parting for the children of Israel to escape from the Egyptian army, and on and on. It sounds so good, just like you think God should be, like you want Him to be. Then, when you are not delivered from evil in some miraculous way, you feel abandoned by God. Why doesn't God come to my rescue? Why do some people receive miracles and I do not? Is there something wrong with my faith? It's a haunting question. It takes a deep faith in God to believe He cares about you in times of suffering. Oh, to have the faith of Job: "Though he slay me, yet will I hope in him" (Job 13:15).

3. God Created Life but Is Not Actively Involved in It

In this position, God is acknowledged as the Creator of life but not as being actively involved in the world or at least in one's personal life. This belief holds that in the beginning God created life but now what happens, happens. You must struggle to make the best of it. You may actually believe in eternal life and yet shut God out of this life. This position holds that God is the beginning and the end but "I" am stuck in the now. It says in effect, "I'm on my own down here. What will be, will be. Good luck!"

Pain Does Not Make Sense

The preceding positions regarding personal pain are common responses from a human perspective. Pain does not make sense. If you believe in God, you can't help but ask the big question: Why? Why would a good God create life in such a way that you will experience pain, grief, and, in the end, death? Indeed, this very question has haunted the minds of philosophers, theologians, and others from the beginning of time. Evil, injustice, and the suffering of the innocent have kept many sincere persons from accepting the basic biblical truism that God is love. God and evil are simply not reconcilable in many people's minds.

CHAPTER 15

CONTRASTING VIEWS OF PAIN

Elie Wiesel

Any attempts to give explanations for human suffering are never satisfying, especially when one has suffered much or has witnessed the brutal suffering of others. Elie Wiesel, author of *Night*, describes terrible scenes of the Holocaust which consumed his father, mother, and little sister. He was just fifteen years of age when he faced the most terrible atrocities imaginable. Along with his family and friends, he was gathered and transported to concentration camps in cattle cars. He describes the dark smoke he saw billowing from a furnace fueled with human flesh as the train pulled into Birkenau. For the first time in his life, Elie smelled the scent of burning flesh. Of that memory he wrote:

> Never shall I forget that night, the first night in camp, which has turned my life into one long night, seven times cursed and seven times sealed. Never shall I forget that smoke. Never shall I forget the little faces of the children, whose bodies I saw turned into wreaths of smoke beneath a silent blue sky.

> Never shall I forget those flames which consumed my faith forever.

> Never shall I forget that nocturnal silence which deprived me, for all eternity, of the desire to live. Never shall I forget those moments which murdered my God and my soul and turned my dreams to dust.

Never shall I forget those things, even if I am con-
demned to live as long as God Himself. Never.[7]

Wiesel tells of the day two adults and a young boy
were hanged at Buna for refusing to disclose information
to the Gestapo. As was the practice, the prisoners were
forced to watch the hangings and then to walk past the
dead and look each one in the face. As Elie watched the
child hanged before him, whose face he described as a sad
angel, he heard a voice behind him ask: "Where is God
now?" Elie heard a voice within him answer, "Where is
He? Here He is—He is hanging here on this gallows. . . ."[8]
That night, he says, the soup tasted of corpses.

"Where is God now?" is a question that plagues many
believers who suffer. Why does God allow evil to devastate
His people? Even for those who do believe in God, it is
still a struggle to understand why injustice, evil, and suffering attack the people of God. It is a perplexing question
without a satisfying answer.

Those who have not suffered much or have not witnessed the ruthless disregard for life in violent acts may not
understand the agony of spirit which causes others to raise
questions about God's existence, His love, or His involvement in the world. In a believer's desire to defend God, it
is easy to give quick answers without participating in the
painful questions. You don't know how you would respond
to a tragedy such as the Holocaust until you would actually
experience its horrors for yourself.

Corrie ten Boom

Then there are others such as Corrie ten Boom, who
was arrested along with her family for concealing Jews in
their home during the Nazi occupation of Holland. She

described Ravensbruck concentration camp as "the deepest hell that man can create." She watched the slow, agonizing death of her sister, Betsie, with whom she shared a deep faith in Christ. Corrie found the strength and grace of God in the midst of her experience and shared that strength with many others. After her sister died, Corrie wrote this moving account of the peace and joy on Betsie's face:

> The Nazi concentration camp was a terrible place. They put the dead bodies into a large washtub. Those who wanted to wash themselves had to step over them. But one day they saw what it meant to be a citizen of heaven—the dead face of Betsie, my sister, was full of heavenly peace and joy, just as the Bible promises.[9]

Corrie and Betsie found meaning in their suffering by bringing the Gospel to many women and ministering God's care to the sick and dying within the camp. They were faithful to Christ in the midst of their suffering. Many of these women found Jesus as a result of their witness and a great number died with the name of the Lord Jesus upon their lips. The day Corrie was released from Ravensbruck, she heard that two of the women whom she had led to Christ had died just that morning. She responded by giving thanks to God for bringing her to Ravensbruck:

> Then I looked at this cruel concentration camp for the last time, and I said: "Thank You, Lord, that You brought me here, even if only for these two women who were saved for eternity, because they found the way to You. You used Betsie and me to that end. Lord, if it were only for these two women, it was worth all our suffering, even Betsie's death."[10]

Corrie went forth from Ravensbruck to proclaim that God is a God of love in whom you can trust. She was called to minister Christ's love, healing, and reconciliation in sixty-four countries during thirty-three years of travel. Great revelations of God's love came from her suffering. She wanted to share what she and Betsie learned in Ravensbruck: "There is no pit so deep that the love of Jesus Christ is not deeper still."

"There is no pit so deep that the love of Jesus Christ is not deeper still."

Your View of Pain

The view that God and suffering are irreconcilable will keep you from seeking God's help and comfort. If God is viewed as a harsh, punishing God, as not caring enough to come to your aid, as distant and removed from your struggles, you will have no incentive to seek Him. Your point of view will place a distance between you and God. You will find yourself terribly alone in a world without God. Feeling abandoned, you may even become angry with God during times of pain and turn from Him. You may see Him as not being available to meet your needs or to comfort you. If God is not available to keep you from evil and pain, you reason, then what is the purpose of believing in God in the first place? How you respond to pain comes down to what you believe about God.

In suffering, then, you are faced with a critical choice: look for a God who is love in the presence of evil or reject the possibility of a God who is love because of evil. It is a very deep and personal search for ultimate truth. It can be an awesome struggle for those who have been ravaged by life. My heart goes out to the many people whose lives have been torn open by the tragedies life brings. I can understand their questions about God's love and protection. I have questioned God's ways in smaller matters. The outcome of the struggle, however, is critical for the soul's survival. You either live on haunted by the dark or you walk on holding on to the Light. You die by your doubts or you live by faith. It's a critical choice that will drive you into the darkness or draw you into the light of knowing Jesus Christ. God has given you the freedom to choose your attitude toward Him.

You either live on haunted by the dark or you walk on holding on to the Light.

PRINCIPLES

---

1. Your reaction to emotional pain will lead to despair or to growth.

2. You can look for the good that pain will accomplish in your life.

3. Pain is not punishment. Pain comes to everyone.

4. Living a righteous life will not shield you from tragedies and pains.

5. In times of suffering, it takes a deep faith in God to believe that He loves you.

6. Pain does not make sense and raises questions about God and His love.

7. The presence of God brings comfort in the darkest of nights.

8. Even while you are suffering, you can minister Christ to those who are hurting.

9. You die by your doubts or you live by faith.

10. The love of Jesus is deeper than the deepest pit.

A REDEMPTIVE RESPONSE TO PAIN

CHAPTER 16

PAIN FULFILLS A PURPOSE

You were created to know God and to love Him. God never intended pain in the first place. He did not intend for pain to destroy you or cause you to question His love. Thus something went awry in God's plan. As the story of the fall explains, Satan entered into the Garden of Eden and destroyed the perfect relationship between God and humankind. Adam and Eve stood in for us when they usurped the authority of God and tried to run their lives their own way. Sin drove Adam and Eve from the Garden and separated them from God. Brokenness, disappointment, and death came into the world because of sin. Thus God did not create evil. Humans brought on evil by their disobedience to God. As we have all learned, there is chaos outside the Garden. That's the bad news.

The good news is that God is actively at work redeeming fallen life. He presented His plan to the world in the person of His Son, Jesus Christ. Jesus came to announce the good news that "whoever believes in Him should not perish, but have everlasting life." In Christ, you see the God who loves, who saves, who has a plan of redemption, who is working on your behalf. Only in Him can the pains of life take on a redemptive purpose.

In Christ, you see the God who is working on your behalf.

God can bring about a particular purpose through your

suffering. It may be to draw you closer to Him, to affect someone else, to work some cause for His good, or to change some area of your life in a way that will fulfill His plan. Whatever the reason, if you are a child of God, God is directing your suffering for His purpose. You do not necessarily need to know that purpose or what God is doing through the suffering. That is God's doing. Your task is to submit yourself to God, allowing Him to use the experiences of your life to fulfill His will in you, and ask Him to give you the faith you need to trust in Him. Peace comes when you stop your strivings and submit your life to God.

There is a subtle danger in this position, however, if you choose a stoic response which removes you from the struggle. You may feel that you must tough it out and endure whatever happens: "Whatever will be, will be." It's almost as if you are not involved in what is happening. This response removes you from the pain of the struggle. It keeps you from asking the hard questions concerning the meaning of this pain. Without a personal involvement in the struggle, without asking how God can help you or use you to work through a painful situation, without looking for what you can learn, there can be no growth. No pain, no gain. This stoic response can shut out God's grace and, as a result, you will miss the meaning of the pain.

If, on the other hand, you choose to view your pain as God working His purpose in you, you will pray for grace to humble yourself before God and earnestly pray that He will use this pain to bring about His will for your life. You submit yourself into His care and surrender to Him. Then you can pray for grace and courage to yield to the will of God and to offer yourself for His purposes, knowing that they may be far greater than you could ever imagine.

The Story of Joseph

Joseph, an Old Testament patriarch, is a prime biblical example of a man of God who submitted himself and the circumstances of his life into the larger care of God's purposes. Beginning in his youth, he experienced a series of evil events. Though beloved by his father, he was rejected by his brothers, sold into slavery in Egypt, falsely accused of attempted rape by Potiphar's wife, and then thrown into jail.

But while in prison, Joseph interpreted a dream of Pharaoh that warned of a serious famine that was coming. Pharaoh was so impressed with Joseph's interpretation that he appointed him to be second-in-command of Egypt. As a ruler, Joseph was able to prepare for the famine.

As the story gains momentum, it reveals the purpose of Joseph's suffering. Many years after Joseph had been sold into slavery by his brothers, the famine spread throughout the region. Joseph's brothers came to Egypt to buy grain. Joseph recognized his brothers and, after a period of testing, revealed his identity to them and offered them forgiveness. Through God's leading in his life, Joseph saved Israel from starvation in order to fulfill God's plan for the nation to give birth to the Saviour of the world, the Messiah. Each situation that appeared to be a serious problem, even an injustice for Joseph, turned out to be a part of the plan of God. Thus Joseph could say to his brothers, "You intended to harm me, but God intended it for good to accomplish what is now being done, the saving of many lives" (Genesis 50:20).

CHAPTER 17

GOD CAN BRING FORTH GOOD

One of the redeeming qualities of painful experiences is that God can bring forth good out of bad situations and use them for His glory. God's redeeming power is able to triumph over the evil of the world and the pain of your life. He turns the cross into an empty tomb. He takes the brokenness of your life and makes it into something beautiful. He turns tears into joys. He breaks and remakes. He creates and then recreates. He takes your pain and turns it into healing and growth. He takes your sin and covers it with His grace. He uses your disadvantages to His advantage. He takes your weaknesses and makes you strong in Him. Through it all He declares, "I am the Lord who heals you" (Exodus 15:26).

God can bring forth good out of bad situations.

Scripture says, "And we know that in all things God works for the good of those who love him, who have been called according to his purpose" (Romans 8:28). This does not mean, as the verse is sometimes interpreted, that God causes or orders evil things to happen for your good. It also does not mean that everything that happens to you is good. The many evils committed daily in the world are certainly not of God. God Himself grieves for the sin, suffering, and brokenness of the world. The cross is the vivid reminder of how seriously God takes the sin and brokenness of this world.

The scripture from Romans says that God works out all things for your good. He moves in your life in such a way that good will be the ultimate outcome of all that happens to you. If God can move through the crucifixion of Christ, release His power through the resurrection, and give new life to those who believe in His Son, then He can do marvelous things with your life. Thus you can look and pray for good to emerge from your painful situations. In times of pain, you can be so blinded by emotional reactions such as grief and anger that you cannot see God or allow Him to work through a situation for good. But the ability of God to do so is there for those who trust Him. The author of Romans tells us that God will have the last word, and it will be good.

CHAPTER 18

GOD WILL PROVIDE A WAY

God holds the resources to see you through painful times. He has ample supplies of grace, strength, and understanding to meet your needs. He stands by you, ready to help. He is Jehovah-jireh, the God Who Will Provide. That was the name Abraham gave to the location where God provided a ram to be sacrificed in Isaac's stead (Genesis 22:14). In the New Testament, the Apostle Paul declares that ". . . my God will meet all your needs according to his glorious riches in Christ Jesus" (Philippians 4:19). Isaiah knew God as One who made a way in the wilderness and streams in the desert (Isaiah 43:19). God will provide a way through the painful times if you seek His help.

Hagar by a Well

The book of Genesis tells the story of Hagar, one that is rich with meaning. Abraham and Sarah were not able to have children even though God had promised that Abraham would be the father of many nations. So Sarah came up with a plan to help God fulfill His promise. She suggested to Abraham that her maid, Hagar, could serve as a surrogate mother and have the child she could not have. Abraham agreed, and Hagar gave birth to a son, Ishmael. Later on, in her old age, Sarah gave birth to a son, Isaac. Isaac and Ishmael were being raised in the same household. The family setting was ripe for major problems. One day Sarah noticed Ishmael mocking her son Isaac. In anger she commanded Abraham, "Get rid of that slave woman and her son, for that slave woman's son will never share in the inheritance with my son Isaac." Abraham faced one of the darkest nights of his soul. He was deeply grieved at Sarah's command, for he dearly loved Ishmael. But God spoke to Abraham and told him to listen to the voice of his wife. So, in great pain, Abraham packed a basket of food, filled a flask with water, and sent Hagar and Ishmael off into the wilderness.

Soon they were lost and without food and water. When they ran out of all their resources and death appeared to be near, Hagar placed her son under a bush and walked away because she could not bear to see him die. Then she lifted up her voice and wept. Ishmael, tired, hungry, fearful, and alone, cried, too.

God heard the cry of Ishmael. He called from heaven and told Hagar not to be afraid. He directed her to lift up her son and take him by the hand, for He would make of him a great nation. Then we read: ". . . God opened her eyes and she saw a well of water. So she went and filled the skin with water and gave the boy a drink" (Genesis 21:19).

Notice that Hagar acted in faith when she took up her son. It was only then that she saw the well. Faith is believing in and then moving on the word of God. Believing is seeing. The story concludes with Hagar and Ishmael joining their people in Egypt.

Faith is believing in and then moving on the word of God.

"God opened her eyes and she saw . . ." The well was there all the time. Her grief, fears, and tears had blinded her from seeing it. God opened her eyes to see the well from which she could draw life. At the very moment when life looked its worst, when it appeared that she and her son would die, when she came to the end of herself, God opened her eyes to see the life-giving resources that were there all the time. The same world that looked so hopeless just a moment before had now become a life-sustaining place. But the Lord had to open her eyes to see what He had provided. God acted to save her. It was a moment of grace, a moment of hope, a moment of life. "For with you is the fountain of life" (Psalm 36:9).

God Opens Your Eyes

In times of sorrow, when it looks as if you have run out of resources, when it seems as if there is no way out, ask God to open your eyes that you may see what He has already provided for you. You see your way through the hard times when God opens your eyes to see what He has already provided. There will be many wells around you from which to draw life. God's abundant grace will sustain you and carry you through the hard places of life. He provides many places to rest and be refreshed. The Apostle Paul encouraged the early believers with these words from Isaiah 64:4: "Eye has not seen, nor ear heard, nor have entered into the heart of man the things which God has prepared for them that love him" (I Corinthians 2:9).

Ask God to open your eyes so you can see what He has already provided for you.

CHAPTER 19

A PLACE OF SPRINGS

The psalmist encourages grieving people who are walking through the Valley of Weeping to find a place of springs where pools of blessings await:

Happy are those who are strong in the Lord,
who want above all else to follow your steps.
When they walk through the Valley of Weeping
it will become a place of springs where pools of
blessing and refreshment collect after rains!
They will grow constantly in strength and each
of them is invited to meet with the Lord in Zion.
— Psalm 84:5-7, TLB

Continuing the Old Testament theme of wells as giving life, Christ spoke to a Samaritan woman by the old well of Jacob one day and told her of the new living water He came to be (John 5). He spoke of "streams of living water" that will flow from within the person who believes in Him. John pointed out that Christ was speaking of the Holy Spirit who lives within each believer (John 7:37-39). Your place of springs from which pools of blessings come is the Spirit of Christ living within your spirit.

Christ's presence within you is your well of life. In His presence you are sustained, comforted, renewed, blessed, and strengthened. Knowing Christ and abiding in His presence is your source of comfort and hope. He is your refreshing place in the hard times.

Christ's presence within you is your well of life.

One day Jesus cried out in a loud voice, "If anyone is thirsty, let him come to me and drink. Whoever believes in me, as the Scripture has said, streams of living water will flow from within him" (John 7:37, 38). Isaiah looked ahead to the coming of the Saviour, the Root of Jesse, and wrote: "With joy you will draw water from the wells of salvation" (12:3).

Walking through the Valley of Weeping is a necessary part of your life, but you will be comforted in knowing that Christ is with you. Your Valley of Weeping can become a place of springs if you see the One who sees you and you draw from His life-giving Spirit within you. Christ is your Fountain of Life. He calls those who are weary and burdened to come to Him and find rest. Christ says, "The water I give him will become in him a spring of water welling up to eternal life" (John 4:14). In the Old Testament, the well is without. In the New Testament, the well is within. If you believe in Christ, the well is within you. Pray that Christ will lead you to know Him as the Fountain of Life.

"For with you is the fountain of life" (Psalm 36:9).

CHAPTER 20

"AS LONG AS I'M WITH YOU"

I was hiking in the woods of a state park one day with my four-year-old granddaughter Lauren. As we walked deeper into the woods, she said to me, "Pappy, are we going to get lost?" I said, "No, we're not going to get lost. We'll just stay on this path and then turn around and come right back on the same path. That way we won't get lost. We'll come back to the place where we started."

We walked along some more and then turned to come back. On the way back we came to a fork in the path. I asked her which way we should go. She pointed up the hill in the wrong direction. I said, "No, if we go that way we might get lost." I led the way on the path that would return us to our starting point.

As we walked along, I teased her about getting lost. I said to her, "You know, if we would have gone up that other path, the way you wanted to go, we might have gotten lost. Then what would you have done?"

She looked up at me with her big, soft, brown eyes and said so sincerely, "Pappy, as long as I'm with you, I would not be lost."

Her remark stopped me in my tracks. "As long as I'm with you, I would not be lost."

I thought of the times I had lost my way on my journey through the wilderness. Times I was lost in fear and anxiety, in depression and anger, in confusion and doubt, in

grief and pain. How much time and energy I had spent trying to get "unlost," trying so desperately to find my way
home. If only I had had faith as a child to look up into my
Heavenly Father's face and say, "As long as I'm with you,
I would not be lost."

CHAPTER 21

PAIN CAN CORRECT YOUR PATH

Sometimes God intervenes in your life to call you to Himself, perhaps even to correct your ways. He arranges or allows pain to enter your life for redemptive purposes. Affliction can be used by God to change the course of your life. It can teach you right from wrong. It can break you so He can remake you. Pain has a way of opening your life to hear God's word. Pain can cause you to re-examine your life and to reflect on the meaning of life. What is important to you? What do you treasure in this life? Where does God fit into the experiences of your life? What keeps you from knowing God? What can you do to experience His healing grace? Pain often drives you to seek God in a renewed way. C. S. Lewis wrote that pain is the megaphone God uses to get our attention.

Pain can open your life to hear God's word.

The psalmist shared how he came to respect the laws of God. He wrote: "Before I was afflicted I went astray, but now I obey your word" (Psalm 119:67). And, "It was good for me to be afflicted so that I might learn your decrees" (Psalm 119:71). Also, "Blessed is the man you discipline, O Lord, the man you teach from your law; you grant him relief from days of trouble . . ." (Psalm 94:12, 13). It is a sad truth that many people go astray until they are afflicted. Then they draw near to God to seek His forgiveness and comfort.

The writer of Hebrews said that Christ, the special Son of God, learned obedience by the things which He suffered (Hebrews 5:8). He wrote of God's discipline. First, he quoted from Proverbs 3:11, 12:

My son, do not make light of the Lord's discipline, and do not lose heart when he rebukes you, because the Lord disciplines those he loves, and he punishes everyone he accepts as a son.

Then he continued with an interpretation of that scripture:

Endure hardship as discipline; God is treating you as sons. For what son is not disciplined by his father? If you are not disciplined (and everyone undergoes discipline), then you are illegitimate children and not true sons. Moreover, we have all had human fathers who disciplined us and we respected them for it. How much more should we submit to the Father of our spirits and live! Our fathers disciplined us for a little while as they thought best; but God disciplines us for our good, that we may share in his holiness. No discipline seems pleasant at the time, but painful. Later on, however, it produces a harvest of righteousness and peace for those who have been trained by it.
— Hebrews 12:7-11

In Revelation 3:19, Christ, the Amen and true witness, says: "Those whom I love I rebuke and discipline. So be earnest, and repent." This scripture describes God as rebuking and disciplining His children that they might get serious about their sins and repent. The biblical word discipline means to guide, to instruct, to lead into maturity, to make a follower of. God's discipline is for your good that you might follow Him and share in His holiness. It's an expression of His love for you.

CHAPTER 22

RECONCILING DISCIPLINE

AND

CHRIST'S TEACHING

How do you reconcile the disciplinary actions of God with the teaching of Christ in Luke 13 that those who experience specific tragedies are no more evil than those who are spared from them?

Place that question within a family context. My wife and I raised four children. There were times when they hurt through no fault of their own. They picked up childhood diseases, hurt themselves falling down, broke bones playing football, needed stitches for cuts, and even, in the case of our older son, required major surgery to correct a heart deformity. These painful situations were not given out as punishment by God upon our children for any particular misdeeds. None of our children was more righteous or more evil than another. Childhood pains are a part of natural life. All children fall learning to walk.

But there were times my wife and I disciplined our children for their own good, to impress on them that particular actions were harmful, even deadly. So we trained them not to wander off on their own when we were shopping or enjoying an amusement park. We did not allow them to ride their bikes on the road until they were ready. We did not allow them to cross the street by themselves at the age of three. They were not allowed to fight with clubs and knives. They were not allowed to drink gasoline. Of course not! To violate any of these rules would, and sometimes did, require discipline. We guided, instructed, and disciplined our children because we loved them.

Painful happenings are not all disciplines from God. Loss is not punishment. Loss happens. But each experience can be used to learn more of God and to grow in faith. In a natural world, there are many tragedies, illnesses, injustices, evils, sufferings, and, eventually, death for everyone. I am no better than my neighbor who suffers from a painful affliction. The rain falls on the just and on the unjust alike. One day I will be the neighbor suffering.

But there are times when God pulls you aside and says, "Wait a minute, My child. Hold it right there! My love for you is too great to allow you to go on like this. I will try to intercept you and turn you around. My love for you demands discipline. I reprove those whom I love. I will deal with you until you change. Your pain will cause you to look to Me. When you look to Me, it is then that I can help you. When you are broken before Me, then I can teach you My laws. I will discipline you because I love you."

**God disciplines out of His love
and care for His children.**

Moses cried out: "Teach me your ways so I may know you" (Exodus 33:13). God's discipline is designed to show you His love and to shape your life for His purposes. It is not punishment for the sake of punishment. When God disciplines, He moves out of love and care for His children.

How can you tell when you are a victim of nature or when you are being disciplined by the Lord? Jesus taught that the Holy Spirit will lead you into all truth. In times of distress and pain, open your heart and ask God what He is doing in your life. What is the purpose of this pain? You are aware that God is at work to fulfill His purpose in your life. He also disciplines those whom He loves. And, as a person of the earth, you will also experience the natural and common difficulties of life. So what is God doing in your life? You look to God for the meaning of your experiences.

One of the keys to spiritual growth is to be open to God's moving in all the events of your life to fulfill a divine purpose. In that belief, you can look for opportunities to grow, witness, and change. You can also look to learn something new about life, God, or yourself that will enrich your life and faith. Thus the issue is not so much why you are suffering as it is being open to God in your suffering.

James looks on the positive side of suffering:

Consider it pure joy, my brothers, whenever you face trials of many kinds, because you know that the testing of your faith develops perseverance. Perseverance must finish its work so that you may be mature and complete, not lacking anything.
— James 1:2-4

CHAPTER 23

PAIN CAN LEAD YOU TO KNOW GOD

God can use the pain in your life to draw you closer to Him. Pain has a way of emptying out the self and making room for God. As you go along, you become so cluttered with the things of this life and so soiled with self that God becomes an abstract concept rather than a comforting person. God seeks you in the hard times that you might know His love for you.

Walking through a painful life situation can cause you to search more deeply to know God. Suffering has a way of deepening the channels through which God's grace often tends to flow unnoticed until it is needed and called upon. Suffering has a way of bringing you to your knees before God. God can work only with a broken and contrite heart.

**God can use the pain in your life
to draw you closer to Him.**

Consider the witness of Jeff. I have known Jeff for about ten years. He was a good man who worked hard, provided well for his family, and helped his neighbors. He did not hesitate to say that he believed in God and that it was important for his children be involved in church. He even went with them occasionally for a special event.

Things were going along quite well for him. Then one day there was an explosion in the mine where he worked. He was knocked unconscious and trapped beneath fallen beams for two hours before he was rescued. He suffered a broken back, his right leg was badly shattered, and a rib penetrated his lungs. It was not known if he would survive.

After seven weeks of intensive care, it was decided to amputate his badly injured leg. Blood clots had cut off all circulation. There was just no other choice, his doctors said. Following therapy at a rehabilitation center for several months, he returned home. His recovery was slow and painful. In a counseling session in which I was helping him and his wife adjust to the changes the accident had brought, I was deeply moved by something he said.

"Not a day goes by," he said, "that I do not thank God for my experience. It brought me to know Him. God became very real to me during this time. In my pain and agony, I found Him or, should I say, I stopped running long enough for Him to find me. I knew He was there all the time, but I never stopped to look for Him until I was flat on my back and forced to look up. Then, when I called out to Him, He came to me and spoke to me. I could feel His presence. For the first time in my life, I knew that He loved me. It was a turning point in my life." Then Jeff spoke the words that deeply moved me: "I can go on without my leg, but I can't go on without my God."

You might never turn to God without the "bumps" that throw you into His arms. Pain calls for relief. Grief calls for comfort. Fear calls for courage. Guilt calls for forgiveness. Weakness calls for strength. Failure calls for assurance. As the old gospel song says: "Where could I go but to the Lord?"

Now, was Jeff being disciplined by the Lord? Or were his injuries an accident? No one really knows. Jeff's response, however, was the key to his spiritual awakening.

Through that experience, Jeff came to know God. God may have planned it for his salvation. What is more important is that God used it for his salvation. It helped to bring about the ultimate purpose of Jeff's life—to know God.

Your response to pain is the key to your spiritual growth.

The question of suffering is larger than looking for possible reasons for it. After all, everyone suffers. Often there is no explanation. Neither can the question simply be asked whether suffering is a punishment for sin or an expression of nature. After all, everyone sins. So it could be argued that all people will be disciplined by God. It is also true that all persons will experience the natural consequences of living in a world plagued with sin, evil, suffering, and death. The most important question is: Are you willing to allow God to use the experiences of your life to do His work in you? Are you willing to seek Him for the faith you need to trust Him? Are you willing to give up your will to His sovereignty? Are you willing to repent of your sins and seek Him with your whole heart? Then, no matter what the reason for the pain, God can work in you and something good will come out of your trials. "For it is God who works in you to will and to act according to his good purpose" (Philippians 2:13). If you allow God to work in your pain, then your painful situations will be used of God for your healing and growth. That belief brings hope. Hope brings endurance. Hope and endurance bring victory.

Philip Yancey, who has done much research on pain and has written several books on God and human suffering, writes:

My anger about pain has melted mostly for one reason: I have come to know God. He has given me joy and love and happiness and goodness. They have come in flashes, in the midst of my confused, unrighteous world, but their presence has been absolute enough to convince me that my God is worthy of trust. Knowing Him is worth all enduring.[11]

CHAPTER 24

CHRIST IS WITH YOU IN THE FLAMES

I love the Old Testament story of the three Hebrew men, Shadrach, Meshach, and Abednego, who refused to obey the king's decree that everyone should bow down and worship a golden image. These Hebrew men worshipped only the one true God, the God of Israel. So they refused to obey the king's decree.

For their punishment, they were thrown into a furnace that was heated seven times beyond its normal heat. The furnace was so hot that the men who threw them in were destroyed by the heat. King Nebuchadnezzar watched all this happening. Then a strange thing happened. Another figure appeared in the flames. The king squinted his eyes and looked intently into the furnace. Who could this be? He said to his men, "Did we not cast three men bound into the midst of the fire? . . . I see four men loose, walking in the midst of the fire; and they are not hurt, and the form of the fourth is like the Son of God" (Daniel 3:24, 25).

Like the Son of God

"Like the Son of God!" Not only were the lives of these three men spared, they did not even smell of smoke. Not only were they released unharmed and praising God, but Christ Himself was with them in the fiery furnace!

A song by the Speer Family tells the story of the three Hebrew men in the fiery furnace. In the song, a child hears this story and asks his mother, "If three went in and three came out, then where did the fourth man go?" The refrain of the song answers the boy's question:

> He's still in the fire,
>   and He's walking in the flame.
> And He'll be there to help you
>   when you call upon His name.
> And He can still deliver
>   by His Almighty Power.
> While here below it's good to know—
>   He's still in the fire.[12]

He's still in the fire with you. He is helping you to face your trial. He is bringing you comfort and hope. He is there to strengthen you, to see you through. He is there to assure you that He is with you. He is there to direct the outcome of your trial. When people ask you how you endured your pain, you can tell them that Christ was with you in the flames. You felt His presence. You knew you were not alone. He delivered you by His grace.

Live or Die—We Will Trust the Lord!

There is a meaningful part of this story of deliverance that is often overlooked. The three Hebrew children made a commitment to totally trust God, live or die! Listen to their response when they were threatened to be burned alive for their faith in God:

> **O Nebuchadnezzar, we do not need to defend ourselves before you in this matter. If we are thrown into the blazing furnace, the God we serve is able to save us from it, and he will rescue us from your hand, O king. But even if he does not, we want you to know, O king, that we will**

not serve your gods or worship the image of gold you have set up.

— Daniel 3:16-18

Do you see the faith of these men of God? They believed God would deliver them from the blazing furnace. But they made it clear that, even if He did not, they would remain loyal to the God of Israel. Their faith was not dependent upon whether or not they were miraculously delivered but upon their God in whom they trusted. Live or die, they would place their trust in Him and live out their faith. They had confidence in God. It's that same deep faith in God that Job found during His suffering: "Though he slay me, yet will I hope in him" (Job 13:15).

Your faith is dependent not upon miraculous deliverances but upon God Himself.

It is this deep faith that brings Christ into your suffering. This confidence believes that God can deliver you from or see you through any trial. It believes that God is with you and loves you and will provide a way through, even if it's not the way you had hoped and prayed for. "So, whether we live or die, we belong to the Lord" (Romans 14:8). It is a sure faith that, no matter what happens, you are in His hands. You belong to the Lord.

"So, whether we live or die, we belong to the Lord."

Christ, describing those who hear His voice and follow Him, said:

I give them eternal life, and they shall never perish; no one can snatch them out of my hand.

**My Father, who has given them to me, is
greater than all; no one can snatch them out
of my Father's hand. I and the Father are one.**

— John 10:28-30

The greatest comfort of the Christian faith is the confidence that you are safe in your Father's hands, that He who loves you will see you through, that His presence gives meaning to your journey, and that His care will guide you safely home. ". . . being confident of this, that he who began a good work in you will carry it on to completion until the day of Christ Jesus" (Philippians 1:6).

CHAPTER 25

SUFFERING REVEALS CHRIST

The story of the three Hebrew children also shows that suffering has the potential of revealing the likeness of the very Son of God who lives within you. He Himself suffered and died to reveal the glory of the Father. Your suffering has the potential of bringing forth the very likeness of the Son of God and revealing His glory, for in your suffering the love and grace of God can be revealed.

Christ can come forth in your love for others, in your patience and suffering, in your courage and endurance, in your faith and hope, even in your weakness. He can take that which hurts the most and turn it into a revelation of Himself. He can take wounds and turn them into revelations of His love, even as His own wounds convinced Thomas of the realness of His suffering. Out of the fiery heat of your trials, Christ can appear.

**Christ can come forth out of the
fiery heat of your trials.**

Fire has a way of burning the dross from you. As the impurities are removed and you go through the cleansing process, as you are brought to your knees before God, God's Spirit begins to do a work of grace in your heart. As you humbly yield to Him in your suffering and offer your pain for His glory, Christ will be revealed in you. The self must be broken and yielded to the glory of God for Christ to be seen. The breaking of the self requires an intense struggle of the soul, similar to what Christ experienced in the garden. Suffering has the potential of bringing forth the Christ in you.

Dear friends, do not be surprised at the painful trial you are suffering, as though something strange were happening to you. But rejoice that you participate in the sufferings of Christ, so that you may be overjoyed when his glory is revealed.

— I Peter 4:12, 13

PRINCIPLES

---

1. In Christ, God is actively at work redeeming fallen life.

2. What appears to be distressing for you may actually be God at work in your life.

3. Christ is with you in your fiery trials.

4. God can bring forth good out of bad situations.

5. God will provide a way through the painful times if you seek Him.

6. Faith is believing in, and then moving on, the promises of God.

7. Christ's presence within you is your well of life.

8. Pain can open your life to know God.

9. God guides, instructs, and disciplines you because He loves you.

10. Suffering has the potential of bringing forth the Christ in you.

11. The greatest comfort of the Christian faith is the confidence that you are safe in your Father's hands.

CHRIST'S RESPONSE TO PAIN

He was despised and rejected by men,
a man of sorrows, and familiar with suffering.
— Isaiah 53:3

CHAPTER 26

HE FACED HIS PAIN

Christ had to deal with much pain in His life. He, too, was acquainted with grief. He was misunderstood, ridiculed, denied, betrayed, scorned, and rejected. His fate was sealed in a rigged and scurrilous trial. He was whipped, nailed to a cross, and humiliated. Thorns were pounded into His head and a sword pierced His side. He was put to an open shame (Hebrews 6:6). He suffered physically, emotionally, and spiritually. He knew the agony of physical torture, the distress of being abandoned, the shame of ridicule, and the spiritual pain of separation from His own Father.

The gospel writer Mark tells of the time Christ was walking with His disciples toward Jerusalem. Jerusalem represented the final destiny of His earthly life. He had already told His disciples that He must suffer much at the hands of the elders, the chief priests, and the teachers of the law. He explained that He would be put to death but three days later He would rise to life. Mark says that He made it very clear to them (Mark 8:31, 32).

It is no surprise, then, that His disciples became alarmed when Jesus turned to go toward Jerusalem, His final place of suffering. Mark says, "They were on their way up to Jerusalem, with Jesus leading the way, and the disciples were astonished, while those who followed were afraid" (Mark 10:32). Jesus was walking into His pain. Luke says that Jesus set His face toward Jerusalem (Luke

9:51, NKJV). Christ led the way to Jerusalem. For Jesus, the way out was the way through. His way to deal with His pain was to turn and face it.

Christ dealt with His pain by turning to face it and walking through it.

CHAPTER 27

HE PRAYED

Christ was a man of prayer. Sometimes He got up early in the morning to find a solitary place where He could pray (Mark 1:35). The Gospel record says that when the crowds began to gather around Him, Jesus often withdrew to lonely places and prayed (Luke 6:12). At times He took His disciples along to pray with Him (Luke 9:28).

> **Very early in the morning, while it was still dark, Jesus got up, left the house and went off to a solitary place, where he prayed.** (Mark 1:35)

He prayed to know His Father's will and for courage to fulfill that will. He prayed that the Father's glory would be revealed through Him. He prayed during the times of His temptations. He prayed for courage to be faithful to His Father's call upon His life. He prayed for His disciples and for all those who would believe in Him. He even prayed for those who persecuted Him. Prayer, that special communion with the Father, gave Him the strength and courage to surrender His life to the will of His Father. The Father's will included His Son's suffering and death.

The Agony of the Garden

Christ's intense struggle in the Garden of Gethsemane revealed the agony of His Spirit. There He struggled with His deepest desire to obey the Father's will. At the same time, He prayed that the cup of suffering would be taken from Him. He was in such agony that He became overwhelmed with sorrow to the point of being near death. As He prayed, He fell on His face to the ground and His sweat was like drops of blood. Again He prayed that this cup would be removed. His real pain was the dying of self to be obedient to the Father's will.

By this time the disciples whom He had brought with Him for comfort and strength were sound asleep. He prayed the third time that the cup might be removed from Him. At the deepest point of His grief, an angel came and ministered to Him and strengthened Him (Luke 22:43). Praying in great intensity and perseverance and strengthened by an angel, He found the strength to yield Himself to the Father's will.

Prayer prepared Christ for His suffering. Prayer broke through His will in order to accept His Father's will. There could be no Calvary without Gethsemane. Prayer brought forth God's sustaining grace in the person of an angel. Prayer prepared Christ to face the cross and bring salvation to the world. God did something better than deliver Christ from the cross. Through His suffering, Christ atoned for the sins of the world and reconciled to the Father those who would accept His sacrifice.

CHAPTER 28

HE EXPRESSED HIS FEELINGS

Christ was aware of His feelings and expressed them openly. He experienced joy and pain, anger and peace, love and disdain. Those close to Him knew what was happening within Him, and they knew where they stood with Him. Today you and I know the thoughts and desires of His heart because He expressed Himself freely and honestly.

Jesus Wept

Jesus felt pain and expressed it openly many times. He wept when He looked over Jerusalem, knowing that the city would be destroyed because the people there did not know the time of their peace (Luke 19:41, 42). He knew the pain of being betrayed and denied by those He loved. He knew the pain of being alone. He knew the pain of facing His suffering and death. The greatest man of faith who ever lived . . . wept.

The greatest man of faith who ever lived . . . wept.

Christ expressed His pain openly from the cross. He expressed His human need when He cried, "I thirst" (John 19:28). In the darkest moment of His life, Jesus experienced the spiritual pain of separation from His Father. He cried out, "My God, my God, why have you forsaken me?" (Matthew 27:46). Jesus, the special Son of God, felt alone and forsaken even by His heavenly Father. He did not feel too special or too proud to express the pain of His heart.

He was not trying to be stoic or succumbing to any need to appear strong. He was responding to the pain of His body and to the agony of His heart as a man.

You catch a glimpse of His broken heart when He stands by the tomb of Lazarus and weeps. Ken Gire, in *Incredible Moments with the Savior*, writes:

> The raising of Lazarus is the most daring and dramatic of all the Savior's healings. He courageously went into a den where hostility raged against him to snatch a friend from the jaws of death.
>
> It was an incredible moment.
>
> It revealed that Jesus was who he said he was— the resurrection and the life. But it revealed something else.
>
> The tears of God.
>
> And who's to say which is more incredible—a man who raises the dead . . . or a God who weeps?[13]

CHAPTER 29

HE IDENTIFIED WITH YOUR PAIN

Christ set forth His mission in life when He proclaimed that the Spirit of the Lord had sent Him "to heal the brokenhearted" (Luke 4:18, NKJV). His earthly life was filled with expressions of compassion as He reached out to touch and heal many with all kinds of diseases (Mark 1:34). The Gospel accounts say that when He saw the sick, He was moved with compassion.

In His identification with those who were hurting, He forgave the woman who was caught in the shameful act of adultery. While others wanted to stone her according to the law, He forgave her according to God's law of grace. He freed the Samaritan woman whom He met at Jacob's well in Sychar from her bondage to male relationships. He healed the man by the pool of Bethesda who had been paralyzed for thirty-eight years. He released Mary Magdalene from the torment of being possessed by seven deamons. He healed lepers who were social outcasts. He healed the lame, the blind, the deaf. He raised the dead!

Jesus identified with those who were hurting.

On the cross, He took upon Himself the sins of the world and the pains of life: "Surely he took up our infirmities and carried our sorrows, . . . But he was pierced for our transgressions, he was crushed for our iniquities; the punishment that brought us peace was upon him, and by his wounds we are healed" (Isaiah 53:4, 5). Christ took upon

Himself the pain of your sin and brokenness. "In all their distress he too was distressed . . ." (Isaiah 63:9). Your heart cannot ache without His aching. He rejoices when you rejoice. He weeps when you weep.

Christ's suffering on the cross reveals the capacity of God to suffer for His creation. The suffering of God through His Son connects Him to those who suffer. From the cross God cried out a groan that resounds throughout time in solidarity with those who suffer. Of Christ's suffering, Philip Yancey writes: "He has joined us. He has hurt and bled and cried and suffered. He has dignified for all time those who suffer by sharing their pain."[14]

Christ has joined you in your suffering.

CHAPTER 30

HE LIVED TO FULFILL HIS FATHER'S WILL

Jesus defined Himself by His relationship with His Father. He said, "I came from God and now am here" (John 8:42). "I am in the Father and the Father is in me" (John 14:11). "I and the Father are one" (John 10:30).

Jesus defined Himself by His relationship with His Father.

Christ's foremost concern was to do the will of the Father. "My food is to do the will of him who sent me and to finish his work" (John 4:34). Later He said, "I seek not to please myself but him who sent me" (John 5:30). "For I have come down from heaven not to do my will but to do the will of him who sent me" (John 6:38).

With a heart set to please His Father, Jesus was in a position to respond openly and honestly to what was happening around Him. He had no need to hide His feelings, to pretend that everything was okay or that everyone was doing just fine. He had no need to deny pain. His acceptance of who He was freed Him from the tyranny of searching for His own personal happiness. His understanding of life was not limited to what felt good in the present. He desired first and foremost to fulfill the Father's plan for His life. He was free to be about His Father's business.

Jesus knew that being faithful to His call would involve pain and suffering. But He also knew that it was not His to be comfortable or to avoid suffering but, rather, to fulfill His Father's will. His suffering served a purpose. It was a part of His commitment to fulfill the mission of His life. The purpose came first; the suffering followed.

Jesus' suffering was a part of His commitment to fulfill the mission of His life.

CHAPTER 31

HE DREW FRIENDS NEAR

Jesus surrounded Himself with friends as He went about His mission. He called twelve disciples to be with Him and to learn from Him. He called them His friends because He shared with them everything that He had learned from His Father (John 15:15). In particular, He chose Peter, James, and John to be His close friends. Jesus took His disciples with Him into the Garden of Gethsemane. Then He chose Peter, James, and John to accompany Him to His special place of prayer. He asked them to stay with Him during this time when His soul was sorrowful and troubled to the point of death (Matthew 26:37, 38). He shared His pain and agony openly with His friends. He wanted their comforting presence.

I have called you friends, for everything that I learned from my Father I have made known to you. (John 15:15)

Jesus loved His friends and they loved Him. His friends brought Him companionship, filled many lonely hours, traveled with Him, laughed with Him, challenged Him, learned from Him, and came to love and serve Him. He loved His disciples and He loved them to the end (John 13:1). His friendship with the disciples prepared them to take on His identity and continue His mission on earth. He was about to lay down His life for His friends, and eventually they would lay down their lives for Him.

CHAPTER 32

HE LOOKED FOR OPPORTUNITIES

It is interesting that Jesus never attempted to explain human suffering. Rather, He accepted the reality of it. In His own ministry, Jesus often used times of adversity to say or do good things. He transformed suffering into something God could use to reveal His grace, either by performing healing miracles or by presenting new ways of thinking about the suffering itself. He used those times to take positive action, to reveal truth, to display the power of God, to draw a parable. Christ was never overcome by adversity. He seized those moments as opportunities to convey some aspect of divine reality.

Christ told His disciples of the suffering the world would experience as the end of the age drew near. He told them of wars, natural catastrophes such as earthquakes, famines, and pestilences, fearful sights, and signs from heaven. Then He warned them of the great suffering that would come to them as they would be persecuted and delivered up to the synagogues and prisons. Their families would betray them, and some of them would even die for their faith. They would stand before kings and rulers for His name's sake (Luke 21).

In the midst of all this predicted calamity, He showed them the opportunities. He said, "This will result in your being witnesses . . . " (vs. 13). Times of suffering can become opportunities to witness for Christ.

One day Jesus met a man who was blind from birth. The disciples asked Him who had sinned, this man or his parents, that he had been born blind. Jesus replied that neither this man nor his parents had sinned. He had been born blind, Jesus said, so that the work of God might be displayed in him. He healed the man and used the event as a witness that He was the light of the world (John 9:1-7).

Times of suffering can become opportunities to witness for Christ.

The suffering of Christ on the cross is the most vivid example of how adversities become opportunities for good. The cross illustrates the deepest injustice that ever happened. But the grace of God turned it into a healing of injustice and sin. Jesus turned the cross into a revelation of His Father's love. Christ's death on the cross at the hands of those who hated Him became life-giving grace to the world. His suffering brought about the redemption of the world. His death was turned into a glorious resurrection. The Victim became the Victor. Christ, "who for the joy set before Him, endured the cross, scorning its shame, and sat down at the right hand of the throne of God. Consider him who endured such opposition from sinful men, so that you will not grow weary and lose heart" (Hebrews 12:2, 3).

Jesus turned the cross into a revelation of His Father's love.

CHAPTER 33

HE FORGAVE

Christ reached a moment of reconciling forgiveness when He prayed from the cross, "Father, forgive them, for they know not what they do." He prayed this prayer in the face of His enemies who mocked Him as He suffered. What a moment of awesome grace and release, of reconciling with the suffering He could not escape, indeed the suffering He was destined to bear. After He offered forgiveness to His enemies, Jesus prepared to surrender His life into His Father's hands.

Forgiveness is the way of making peace with God, with others, with self, with life, with suffering, with injustices—yes, even with death. Christ knew the peace and release of forgiveness. He surrendered the injustices He had suffered to divine forgiveness. He prepared to surrender all of His suffering into the Father's hands. His final reconciliation with the realities of life and death had come.

CHAPTER 34

HE KNEW HIS FUTURE WAS SECURE

Jesus knew His future was secure in His Father's hands. That knowledge freed Him from the tyranny of the fear of pain. It was Christ who taught His disciples not to worry about tomorrow (Matthew 6:34) but rather to trust their heavenly Father to meet their needs day by day.

Jesus declared: "I came from the Father and entered the world; now I am leaving the world and going back to the Father" (John 16:28). He knew His beginning and His end. No amount of pain or humiliation would change His identity or His future.

**Jesus knew His future was secure
in His Father's hands.**

Jesus knew that pain was not His ultimate enemy. He would rise above it in the end. He could face pain because He knew it was temporary. He had to endure pain in order to fulfill the purpose of His life on earth. He accepted His pain as a part of His life and ministry. But He also knew that neither pain nor death itself could defeat Him. The purposes of God were larger than His pain. His pain would be used of God to bring about the Father's will for His life and the life of the world. Thus pain was not His stopping place. It was the atonement for the sins of the world that He was called to bear. His death on the cross would lead to the new life of the resurrection. He trusted His Father to have the last word, and He knew it would be good!

The Resurrection Gives Hope

In the midst of His trial before the Sanhedrin, Jesus said: "In the future you will see the Son of Man sitting at the right hand of the Mighty One and coming on the clouds of heaven" (Matthew 26:64). Surrounded by enemies who wanted Him dead, Jesus kept His heart fixed on His purpose. He looked beyond His present pain to see His future glory!

"In the future!" Christ knew He had a future. He spoke confidently of His own resurrection from the dead. In view of His resurrection, no pain in life could defeat Him. He would outlive His pain and rise above it in the end. Death was not the final enemy of His life; rather, it was a part of His entrance into a new life. It was something He had to pass through in order to complete His mission and be with His Father. ". . . who for the joy that was set before Him endured the cross, despising the shame, and has sat down at the right hand of the throne of God" (Hebrews 12:2, NKJV).

**In view of His resurrection,
no pain in life could defeat Him.**

CHAPTER 35

HE SURRENDERED TO THE FATHER

Christ came to that awesome moment of complete surrender to the Father. He could not escape His suffering and death. He was on the cross. His only hope was His faith in a heavenly Father who loved Him. His earthly life was ending. He cried out, "Father, into Your hands I commit my spirit." Then He died.

Christ did not come to that place without an intense struggle. Gethsemane was a time of surrender. In the Garden He laid down His life to be obedient to the Father. He placed His life into His Father's hands. As He lived, so He died. He trusted His Father to fulfill His promise to Him. His final place would be with His Father. Being with His Father was the destiny of His life, the longing of His heart, the hope of His future. All of that which He believed, taught, and lived came to rest in His Father's hands. His final word from the cross was His final view of life—trust in His Father's care.

PRINCIPLES

---

1. Jesus knew pain and expressed it openly.

2. Christ dealt with His pain by facing it and walking through it.

3. Prayer prepared Christ for His suffering.

4. The greatest man of faith who ever lived . . . wept.

5. Christ identifies with your pain.

6. Jesus defined Himself by His relationship with His Father.

7. In Gethsemane, Jesus surrounded Himself with His friends.

8. Jesus turned the cross into a revelation of His Father's love.

9. Jesus surrendered the injustices of the cross to divine forgiveness.

10. Jesus looked beyond His pain to see His future glory.

11. Jesus knew His future was secure in His Father's hands.

12. Jesus trusted His Father to have the final word. He knew it would be good!

YOUR RESPONSE TO PAIN

Jesus, thou art all compassion,
Pure unbounded love thou art.
Visit us with thy salvation,
Enter every trembling heart.
— John Wesley

CHAPTER 36

FACING YOUR PAIN

Christ walked the path of life and experienced it as you and I do. He knew human suffering and faced His own sorrows. He found the strength to face life and keep focused on His mission. He looked for opportunities to reveal God's grace in the midst of evil. He was not overcome by evil but overcame evil with good. As your Saviour, teacher, example, and elder brother, He pioneered a new way to look at life's pains and face its challenges. Thus you can learn from Him, grow through Him, and press on in Him. He is the Way, the Truth, and the Life sent from the Father to lead you through life on your journey home. You can learn to deal with your pain by the way Christ dealt with His pain.

You can learn to deal with your pain by the way Christ dealt with His pain.

When the time came for Christ to face the final pain, He began His journey toward Jerusalem. He walked into His pain. To turn and face your pain is distressing. How you wish you could wake up and discover it is merely a bad dream! You want to look for a way out rather than a way through. Christ found the inner strength to "set His face toward Jerusalem." His presence with you encourages you to face your pain and to look for strength to find the way through. He has already made His journey. Now He joins you on your journey.

138 @ Tears In a Bottle

Jesus faced His suffering by acknowledging it and talking about it. He prepared Himself by seeking the presence of His Father. He told His disciples very plainly that they, too, would know trouble and sorrow: "In this world you will have trouble. But take heart! I have overcome the world" (John 16:33).

Christ is with you in your place of suffering. He walks with you on your journey. He is familiar with sorrow and grief. He knows the pain you are facing. He walks with you through your pain. He desires to carry your burdens and give you rest. Through His own suffering, He found the strength to endure to the end. He overcame the world and defeated the power of sin and death. In speaking of the disciples' suffering, Christ said to them: "I have told you these things, so that in me you may have peace" (John 16:33). "For just as the sufferings of Christ flow over into our lives, so also through Christ our comfort overflows" (2 Corinthians 1:5).

The real question is not why you are suffering, whether or not you should be suffering, or how much you are suffering. The real question is, "Are you coming into God's comfort?"

CHAPTER 37
PRAYER

Prayer is the desire and communication of the heart to be one with God. It is your greatest resource in dealing with pain. Prayer unites your heart with God's heart in a special spiritual relationship that becomes the most powerful of all the healing forces. You can draw faith, hope, and strength from this special relationship with God.

Praying when you are hurting is difficult yet healing. Prayer helps to release your pain to God who loves you and understands your needs. When you are hurting, there is a childlike yearning for comfort. Tears may flow freely as you express your feelings. There may be deep groaning of the soul as you pour out your heart to God. Many troubled souls have known the peace that has come after they have poured out their hearts to God. Prayer touches the heart of God and releases His power and healing grace. The psalmist said, "Trust in him at all times, O people; pour out your heart to him, for God is our refuge" (Psalm 62:8).

Prayer touches the heart of God and releases His power and healing grace.

I have found prayer to be most helpful to get through a hard time. I pour out my heart to God, affirm my faith in Him, ask for His mercy and grace, and place the situation into His hands. It doesn't always resolve the situation, but it gives me strength and hope. I have Someone to hold on to, and I become aware of Someone holding on to me.

Prayer Looks to Your Hope

A man told me of his experience of caring for his aged and ill mother. This very stressful situation consumed his time and energy. He didn't know how long he could continue to provide the care she needed. He felt guilty about his feelings of helplessness and their accompanying frustration and anger.

We talked about prayer and its effect upon us. He said, "When I pray, I feel so much better. I feel at peace. I don't understand it, but it gives me the strength to go on."

Prayer did not change his situation. It did not restore his mother's health. It did not give him more hours in the day or pay the medical bills. So how was prayer helping him? We concluded that prayer diverted attention from the problem so that he could focus his hope on God. "For in you, O Lord, I hope; You will hear, O Lord my God" (Psalm 38:15, NKJV).

Prayer looks to God for help. Comfort doesn't come from understanding the "why" of suffering. Comfort comes from drawing close to the heart of God. Hope comes from trusting in the promises of God. Prayer comforts you, for you are now in touch with the source of your hope. Hope brings comfort, and comfort brings strength. Your hope and strength are in God. "God is our refuge and strength, an ever present help in trouble" (Psalm 46:1).

**Comfort comes from drawing close
to the heart of God.**

Prayer Surrenders to God

Prayer is an opportunity to ask for God's grace to surround a painful happening. In prayer, you ask for courage and strength to face the pain, praying that you will be found faithful. You ask God to show you the way through, believing that His grace will be revealed through your suffering and affirming that He will use this situation for good. Prayer surrenders your pain to the will and way of God in your life. One of the most difficult prayers you can ever pray is to ask God to take your suffering and turn it into a blessing for yourself and others, in the end honoring and glorifying Himself.

**Prayer surrenders your pain to the will
and way of God in your life.**

My heart is drawn to Stephen, the first Christian martyr of the New Testament Church. As he was being stoned to death by an angry mob, he asked God to forgive them and prayed for the Lord Jesus to receive his spirit. We have no record that he pled for mercy or asked to be delivered from this horrible death. Stephen's cry was a real prayer of relinquishment, of letting go and trusting God. He looked up and saw Jesus standing at the right hand of God (Acts 7:54-60). He took the prayers Jesus prayed from the cross and made them his own.

When we look at the world we are distressed;
When we look at ourselves we are depressed;
When we look at God we are at rest.
— Corrie ten Boom

CHAPTER 38

EXPRESSING YOUR FEELINGS

Much time and energy are spent trying to avoid or conceal pain. How quickly you can "tuck it all in," tell yourself it doesn't really matter, and put on a stoic front. You may do rash things to deny the pain. When pain is not faced and dealt with, it never gets to do its work in your life. It is not given the opportunity to be surrounded by God's healing grace. Christ faced His pain and expressed it openly and honestly. He allowed those around Him to see His heart and to feel His pain. By living openly and honestly, He showed them the heart of the Father.

His presence in your life encourages you to face pain and to express it openly. Recognizing His humanness helps you to face your own humanity. Releasing pain openly and honestly keeps your feelings flowing and prevents them from damming up within you, causing upheavals of negative energy. Dammed-up feelings keep you from knowing the flow of God's grace in your life. God's healing grace will flow in as you release the pain inside you. Expressing your pain opens the way for God to enter into your struggle in order to bring forth His redemptive purpose. You don't want to miss the meaning of your pain.

CHAPTER 39

OFFERING YOUR WOUNDS

Jesus did not try to hide the wounds of His life. He bled openly and cried out loudly. He submitted His wounds for His Father's redemptive purposes. It's in His brokenness that you find your wholeness. "This is My body, which is broken for you" (I Corinthians 11:24, NKJV).

God can use your wounds to work His ministry of healing through you. It is healing for others to see and feel your wounds and to hear the cries of your heart. Others understand pain. They hurt, too. You may want to hide your pain because you feel the need to be strong and in control of your life. You may have accepted the belief that to cry is to be weak, to ask for help is to be inadequate, to seek friendship with others is to be vulnerable, to be vulnerable is to be abused. So you grin and bear the pain and tough it out as long as you can. But expressing your pain and offering it to God for His purpose gives God the opportunity to use those wounds to reveal Himself to the world.

God can use your wounds to work His ministry of healing through you.

You may feel that you need to have it all together in order to be an effective witness for God or else your testimony will be flawed. You try to deny pain as much as you can so you can be used of God. You may feel the need to be strong so you can be a strong witness. How can God use me when I am broken? you may ask. When I don't under-

144 @ Tears In a Bottle

stand His ways myself? When I have questions and doubts? When I feel weak and inadequate? But then you discover a challenging truth in Scripture. God does His work through His broken earthen vessels. By working through you when you feel inadequate and unworthy, broken and wounded, sad and discouraged, He shows you that in your weakness He is strong in you (II Corinthians 12:10). God can use your pain to open your heart to the pain of others. You can become a healer even in your woundedness if you offer your broken vessel to God for His use and for His glory.

CHAPTER 40

WOUNDS WILL CHANGE YOU

You never come through a wounding encounter the same way you entered it. It leaves its mark upon you. The wounds of Christ were visible following His resurrection. He showed the disciples His wounded hands and side. When Thomas saw the wounds of Jesus, he believed. They were just too real. A gospel song says, "I will know Him by the prints of the nails in His hands." They are wounds of redemption, marks of victory, imprints of salvation.

The wounds of life will change you if you allow God to work within you. Your wounds can become times of growth, marks of redemption, imprints of victory. And God's will is accomplished in your life once again—through your brokenness and suffering.

**The wounds of life will change you
if you allow God to work within you.**

If you allow God to minister His grace to you during times of suffering, you will learn much about God's grace and His sustaining power. You will be less fearful of the future, for you will have met the God whose presence sustains and comforts you. You will be more ready to face the day, for you will have already borne the heat of the day. Suffering reveals your inadequacies and God's adequacies. You will begin more and more to trust God to be in control of your life. You will begin to relinquish your desires to His grace. You will find that He is the God who comforts, sustains, and provides. He is the God you have come to know and trust. He is the God whose strength you have experienced. He is the God who comforts you in all your distress. He is the God who will lead you into the future He has for you. In that awareness, you can now reach out to care for the wounds of others more tenderly and compassionately, for you have met the God who heals.

I met Amber Walker, a seventeen-year-old, at a local Christian Writers' fellowship. She wrote a moving story about a scar she bears as a result of open-heart surgery at the age of five. In her teens, she became increasingly conscious of her scar and tried to keep it covered. One day, in hot tears of anger, she cried out to God, "I hate this scar!" At this point, I want to pick up the story in her own words:

> God then spoke to me. Not in His small soft voice at first, but with a mental image of Jesus on the cross. Then His voice whispered to my heart, "Is a scar such a terrible thing to have?" It then hit me. The back lashed by a Roman's whip, the wrists and feet bored into by huge, crude nails, the brow pierced into by a savage crown of thorns. His side, stabbed by a spear.

> A lump nestled itself into my throat, and God spoke to my heart once more. "If you did not have your scar, you would have no life. If I did not have My scars, you would have no hope."

> I never thought about it like that. I knew that Jesus was wounded for our transgressions, but I had never thought about the scars. My tears of anger turned to tears of humility, and I bowed my head with shame. The burden of my scar was raised and, ever since, I have been looking at my scar in a new light.

My spiritual mentor once said, "Sometimes we get so wrapped up in the immediate we forget the permanent." Why, this scar was immediate now. But it was not permanent! When I die, I'll go to heaven with a new body! No scars!

A few weeks later I bought a Christian CD and the Lord gently confirmed His words to me about my heart through the song of the Christian artist Carman. The verse of the song is my encouragement today, and if I ever look down on my scars again, this song's words will ring my heart.

Jesus Christ was wounded, too
With wounds deeper than ours.
That's why no child of God
Should ever be embarrassed by their scars.[15]

CHAPTER 41

IDENTIFYING WITH THOSE IN PAIN

Followers of Christ are called to identify with those who suffer. The pain He bore for others becomes the pain you bear for others. In the spirit of Christ you take upon yourself the pains of life by working for the relief of human suffering in whatever form it is found. You "mourn with those who mourn" (Romans 12:15) and remember those who suffer as if you shared their pain (Hebrews 13:3). In your identity with Christ, you are now embarking on a journey to offer Christ's healing to those who suffer. The Father did not send you to the earth to live a painless and easy life. Rather, He sent you to continue the ministry of Christ "to heal the brokenhearted." Suffering with and for others is the indelible mark Christ left upon the hearts of His followers. Your mission in life is to continue the mission of Christ.

Your mission in life is to continue the mission of Christ.

When you offer yourself for the healing of the world, you enter into both the depth and the agony of God's love. You become one with Christ as He calls you to suffer for the redemption of the world. As the great Apostle Paul experienced: ". . . I bear on my body the marks of Jesus" (Galatians 6:17). These are marks of redemption, of grace, and of healing, marks of identifying with the pains of the world, marks of identifying with Jesus.

Wounded healers are used of God to bring healing to others. The balm of acceptance, understanding, and compassion bonds wounded spirits together in a healing embrace. Christ extended that grace from the cross to those who suffer. "By His stripes we are healed." Offering yourself to a suffering world imprints the marks of Jesus upon you. Or, as a friend said to me, do we not offer ourselves because we have already been imprinted?

Those who have suffered much have the greatest compassion for others. "It was in those who recovered from the plague," wrote Thucydidas, "that the sick and the dying found the most compassion." Ernest Hemingway wrote that "life breaks us all and afterward many are strong at the broken places." God prepares you to minister to a hurting world by leading you through the griefs and sorrows of your own life. The Apostle Paul writes that God comforts us in all our troubles "so that we can comfort those in any trouble with the comfort we ourselves have received from God" (2 Corinthians 1:4). In the hands of God, the cause of your greatest pain can become the source of your greatest blessing.

In the hands of God, the cause of your greatest pain can become the source of your greatest blessing.

Patsy Clairmont wrote:

The God of all comfort does not seem to extend His comfort to make us comfortable. Perhaps that's because our tendency would be to become La-Z-Boy believers, content to crank back our chairs, put up our feet, and snooze through the losses of others.

Instead, He offers His comfort that we might be motivated by mercy to tenderly extend kindness to the hurting. . . .

If we don't feel, weep, talk, rage, grieve, and question, we will hide and be afraid of the parts of life that deepen us. They make us not only wiser but also gentler, more compassionate, less critical, and more Christlike.[16]

CHAPTER 42

SERVING GOD

If you believe that your purpose in life is to find security and happiness, you set yourself up for continual disappointment. You will never be satisfied. You will always want more. You will spend a lifetime searching for what you don't have and think you need. Some of your pain in life comes from wanting things that you cannot have. I remember hearing a great truth that challenged me: "If you want to be healed where you hurt the most, you have to be willing to give up that which you want the most."

"If you want to be healed where you hurt the most, you have to be willing to give up that which you want the most."

If, on the other hand, you live to fulfill God's design for your life and you work with Him to accomplish His work, you become involved in an ultimate purpose that gives meaning to the present moment and hope to the future. Christ found His meaning and purpose when He broke through self to pray to His Father, "Here I am, I have come to do your will" (Hebrews 10:9). You can find that meaning, too, if you offer your body as a living sacrifice, holy and pleasing to God, and desire to serve in the same spirit of His Son, Jesus Christ. Then you will have a mission to fulfill in life. The mission may at times be painful to carry out. You must be freed from serving self before you are free to serve Christ. But you have this promise:

"Those who sow in tears will reap with songs of joy" (Psalm 126:5). The greatest comfort in life is knowing Jesus Christ. The greatest joy in life is serving Jesus Christ!

CHAPTER 43

KNOW WHO YOU ARE IN CHRIST

Your identity is in Christ. "For in Him we live and move and have our being" (Acts 17:28). Suffering gains meaning when you know who you are in Christ. As Christ was not alone in His suffering, neither are you alone in your suffering. He suffers with you because He lives in you. Your suffering becomes His, too. In that oneness, in that intimate relationship with Him, you find the purpose of all of your days—the good ones and the bad ones: "Christ in you, the hope of glory" (Colossians 1:27). Knowing who you are in Christ gives you an identity and a security that helps you to cope with life and its pain. His Spirit dwells within your spirit. Thus His strength becomes your strength, His peace your peace.

In times of loss and grief, remember who you are!

Identity with Christ brings meaning to your struggles and sufferings. You are first and foremost a child of God. Of His followers, Jesus said: "I give them eternal life, and they shall never perish; no one can snatch them out of my hand" (John 10:28). Your identity as God's child brings comfort, hope, and strength. Nothing can ever change your identity as God's special child. He has written your name on the palms of His hands (Isaiah 49:16), and you are His. Nothing can ever separate you from His love. In times of loss and grief, remember who you are!

CHAPTER 44

BORN INTO A NEW FAMILY

Christ looked down from the cross in the midst of His awesome pain and suffering and saw His mother and John standing nearby. He understood their pain and grief. He knew that both of them would be in need of care and comfort. "When Jesus saw his mother there, and the disciple whom he loved standing nearby, he said to his mother, 'Dear woman, here is your son,' and to the disciple, 'Here is your mother.' From that time on, this disciple took her into his home" (John 19:26, 27).

Christ recognized and met the need for the comfort of His family and friends. A new family was created at the cross, a family that now draws its comfort from a shared faith and hope in Christ. By their love for Christ and for one another, they build a spiritual home on this earth in which they serve Christ and each other.

God created a spiritual home for you on this earth while He prepares an eternal home for you. Your spiritual home is a place to be comforted, to be loved, to be forgiven, to be healed. The new family of faith that gathers around the cross is called to help create that spiritual home by caring for one another and offering the comfort, grace, and peace of God. You are called to enter fully into that family and become a vital part of its growth and well-being by offering the comfort and peace of Christ to others.

CHAPTER 45

OPPORTUNITIES IN ADVERSITY

During the years that I served as a pastor, I was often moved by the witness of those who were suffering and approaching death. I will always remember a man named Jack. He worked in the steel mill. He was a big, strong man and a great hunter and fisherman. Shortly after he retired from the mill, he was diagnosed with cancer and began a painful time of suffering. I saw him just before he died. On that day he said to me, "I always believed in God, but lately Christ has become so real to me. I didn't know I could have such close fellowship with Him. I wish it had not taken so long for me to know Him. Most of my life I believed in Him, but only recently have I really come to know Him. If I had known Christ earlier in my life, I would have been a different man. He has come to me and I have learned to trust Him. I have seen the Lord. If this is what it took for me to know the Lord in this life, then I would not exchange anything for it. I know now that I will soon be with Him and everything will be okay."

His testimony of God's nearness during his time of suffering left a lasting impression on me, his family, and his friends. The certainty of his faith was convincing. I thought to myself, "Wow, if I could just find that kind of faith now!" I was determined to seek God now and not wait until my last days. Jack used his suffering as a testimony. The greatest testimony of his life came at the end. "This will result in your being witnesses . . . " (Luke 21:13).

Examples of those who use their suffering as a testimony are many. Recovering alcoholics use their experiences to help other alcoholics find hope. Recovering abuse victims become advocates at help centers. People who have lost children form support groups for grieving parents. Parents of special-needs children call on parents who are in shock following the birth of a handicapped child and stand alongside them. A convicted felon who has found a new life in Christ leads a Bible study for prisoners. A pastor recovering from burnout starts a support group for pastors who wish to stay healthy. The list of ways to turn adversities into opportunities is endless. Indeed, sufferings turned into testimonies are marvelous witnesses of God's amazing grace.

Life will give you many opportunities to be a witness in suffering. If you believe that God is at work directing your life, fulfilling His will for you through the events of your life, and promising to bring good to those who love Him, then you, too, can look for opportunities to be a witness for Christ. Your sufferings can become times for Christ to be revealed through you, times for sharing your faith, times for trusting more deeply in God, times for healing and growth, times for reaching out to others in love. As suffering draws you closer to the heart of God, your testimony becomes deeper and more pronounced. Witness can be given to the Christ who suffered for the redemption of the world.

**Life will give you many opportunities
to be a witness in suffering.**

CHAPTER 46

FORGIVENESS

The injustices of life are often difficult to forgive. When life isn't fair, you hurt deeply and may complain bitterly. Pain cries out for justice, for answers, for revenge. "Why should I suffer like this?" you may cry. "Look at all the unrighteous people around me who are prospering. It's not fair!"

Three recent visits to victims of cancer raised painful questions for me. One man has been retired for 14 years and now faces prostate cancer that is spreading to surrounding lymph nodes. He has completed radiation and chemotherapy. There is no further treatment. He sat across from me and said, "I'm grateful for the good years God has given me, but it's getting harder and harder. I'm beginning to lose control of my life. And I'm so tired—so tired. I don't understand why I am suffering this way."

In another pastoral visit I tried to console a young mother of three children who had just lost her husband to cancer. Within six weeks of the diagnosis he was gone, just like that! The woman was still in shock. "I'll never understand why my husband had to die so young," she said. "It isn't fair. It just isn't fair."

Then I drove out of town to visit a seventy-year-old precious saint of God who barely recognized me. The ravaging cancer was rapidly ending her life. I tried to talk with her. Occasionally she responded in a limited way. But when I began saying the 23rd Psalm she began to say the

words with me. Softly I began singing "Jesus Loves Me."
With tears sliding down her cheeks, she joined in. We sang
and cried together. A brief prayer committed her life into
God's care. I left her bedside, got into my car, and
slammed my fists onto the steering wheel. "God," I cried,
"it isn't right. It just isn't right! She is one of Your children! I don't understand why she is suffering this way! I'm
so grateful she knows You. She'll soon be with You. But
why all this suffering now?" I just sat there and cried.

**Forgiveness is the ultimate expression of faith
in God and in His goodness.**

Life brings all of us to times of unanswered questions,
times when the wrongs cannot be made right on this earth,
when the injustices wear us down. Through Christ's prayer
from the cross, "Father, forgive them, for they know not
what they do," we become aware that injustice and doubts
can be released through the experience of forgiveness.
There are times for forgiving life its injustices, for releasing resentment toward God for "allowing this to happen to
me," for forgiving the enemies who are robbing you of
life's joys, and for releasing your questions into God's
care. At those moments, you begin to reconcile your inner
struggles with life to an awareness of your need for God's
grace to forgive. Sometimes you can only receive healing
for life's hurts by offering forgiveness to whomever or
whatever has injured you. One of the last things that Jesus
did on the cross was to forgive His enemies. Forgiveness is
the ultimate expression of faith in God and in His goodness. It is the ultimate expression of healing.

CHAPTER 47

SURRENDERING TO GOD

There are times in life when you do your best to deal with pain. You cry out to the Lord to deliver you from some terrible ordeal. But God does not rescue you. He allows you to struggle on. Eventually the human struggle ends in death. You sense it, you feel it, you know it happens to everyone. But it's so painful to come to that point of surrender, to give up the fight, and to rely on the mercy of God to see you through. In some ways, throughout your lifetime you prepare for this moment of death, yet you are never ready to accept it or to enter into it without protest and denial. But it comes. It just comes.

In painful times, you don't understand the ways of life, much less the ways of God. Things happen from which you see no redeemable benefits. Evil seems to triumph too often. Unexplainable tragedies happen to God's people. Why do some suffer while others prosper?

You know the agony of your questions, the emptiness of loneliness, and your unrelenting search for answers. Desiring to love and serve a God whose ways you don't understand presses you to new levels of trust. At those times, you are forced to die your deaths in this life and surrender to the sovereignty of God. This calls you to surrender your pain, your questions, and your doubts. Surrendering to God says, "God, You know best. I want You to be in control of my life. I cannot see what You are doing, but give me the faith to believe that You know what You are doing. Do what is best in spite of my protest and questions. Do what You need to do to bring good out of this evil. You are God. Ultimately I must trust You with my life. I want to learn to trust You now."

CHAPTER 48

LETTING GO

It is so painful to let go of that which gives you love, security, and meaning. Yet, from birth to death, life is filled with many "letting go" experiences—sometimes temporary, sometimes permanent. The pain of letting go forces you to face the reality that a great loss has occurred. Pain forces you to move from where you want to be to where reality is now calling you to be. It propels you to take action, to begin the process of letting go, to move along the path of reality, to think differently about the future. Pain helps you to let go of the things of this life so you can hold on to the things of God more surely. You should not become so attached to anything on this earth that you cannot go on and serve God without it. If your security is based on things that can be taken from you, you will be living in a constant state of anxiety, always vulnerable to changes and losses. Pain teaches you that, like Christ, you will eventually come to the end of your life and find ultimate release ("letting go") by committing your spirit into the hands of God. Letting go of the things that you are called to let go of in this life prepares you for your final time of letting go and trusting God.

Pain helps you to let go of the things of this life so you can hold on to the things of God.

Elisabeth Elliot, in her devotional book *A Lamp For My Feet*, writes that Paul counted his losses to be pure gain. She writes that the key to transforming earthly losses into heavenly gains is to love God above all else.

> What do we love? If our hearts are set on people and possessions and position, the loss of those will indeed be irreparable. To the man or woman whose heart is set on Christ no loss on earth can be irreparable. It may shock us for the moment. We may feel hurt, outraged, desolate, helpless. That is our humanity. But the Lord can show us the "long view," the incalculable gain in spiritual and eternal terms, if we love Him above all. Everything that belongs to us belongs also to Him. Everything that belongs to Him belongs also to us. What, then, can we *finally* lose? If we lose not Christ Himself, we have finally lost nothing, for He is our treasure and He has our hearts.[17]

Mother Theresa said, "You will never know that Jesus is all that you need until Jesus is all that you have."

CHAPTER 49

LIVING FOR THE FUTURE

Jesus spoke the most revolutionary words ever spoken: "Because I live, you also will live" (John 14:19). The assurance of your resurrection gives you a hopeful perspective from which to view life and its suffering. All suffering passes. Nothing is permanent on this earth. A familiar gospel song says, "This world is not my home, I'm just a passing thru." Christians are living for the future. You will outlive your pain. You die your deaths in this life in anticipation of the resurrection. In the midst of the pains of this life you set your heart toward home for "the joy set before you." God created you both for this life and for eternity. Through the eyes of faith you can look beyond your present suffering to see your future glory. "I consider that our present sufferings are not worth comparing with the glory that will be revealed in us" (Romans 8:18).

The 'Now' of the Resurrection

The power of the resurrection is available in the present moment to raise you up from the hard knocks and dead ends of life and give you hope. As you die many deaths in this life, so you can experience many resurrections as you wait for the final and complete resurrection. Consider this powerful spiritual truth:

And if the Spirit of him who raised Jesus from the dead is living in you, he who raised Christ from the dead will also give life to your

mortal bodies through his Spirit, who lives in you.

—Romans 8:11

I stopped in amazement one day when I saw this great truth of the resurrection. The same Spirit who raised Christ from the dead dwells in me. Really! I came to see this great, life-changing truth that the resurrrection is also for this moment! Christ lives in you now and gives life to both your spirit and your mortal body. The Spirit of the resurrection dwells in you to give you life, to raise you back up after you've been knocked down, to give you hope when you are in despair. You are replenished when you've been drained, renewed in faith when you feel like giving up, restored in times of exhaustion, and healed when you've been crushed. You are given life when you want to die.

**The same Spirit who raised Christ
from the dead dwells in you.**

If the same Spirit who raised Christ from the dead dwells in you, there is hope for every situation you will ever face, no matter how painful or defeating. Yes, you will be knocked down many times in life but, just as Christ rose again, you will, too. As you die your deaths in this life, you will rise again and again by the Spirit of Christ living in you. You may cry out in agony and wonder where God is when life deals you a hard blow. But after you have let go, after you have done your dying and committed your spirit into God's hands, you will rise again! Death cannot keep you in the ground. The power of the risen Christ will lift you up and give you life. In *Suffering Into Joy*, Mother Theresa says, "Never let anything so fill you with pain or sorrow, so as to make you forget the joy of Christ risen."[18]

The Hope of the Resurrection

The hope of the resurrection gives a future look to life. No matter how long or hard or dark the night, there is a future. A better day is coming. Life takes on a different view from the empty tomb. In the Christian faith, hope keeps believing, pressing on, looking ahead to what is promised. Hope keeps you from focusing just on the painful times and lifts you beyond the present pain to see a new day coming. That perspective takes the hopelessness out of your dark nights, for it is when you become hopeless that you suffer the most. Hopelessness is a disease of the soul that traumatizes the spirit. It is deadly because it keeps you swirling around in your pain. It keeps you from seeing a way through the present darkness. Without hope, the soul lacks the energy to get up in the morning or to believe that a better day is coming. You are blessed with hope's healing when you take the circumstances of this life and place them into the perspective of the resurrection.

Life takes on a different view from the empty tomb.

PRINCIPLES

---

1. You can learn to deal with your pain by the way Christ dealt with His pain.

2. Christ is with you in your place of suffering.

3. Comfort comes from drawing close to the heart of God.

4. The wounds of life will change you if you allow God to work within you.

5. In the hands of God, the source of your greatest pain can become the source of your greatest blessing.

6. In times of loss and grief, remember who you are.

7. Christ can be revealed in your suffering.

8. Forgiveness is the ultimate expression of faith in God and in His goodness.

9. Pain helps you to let go of the things of this life so you can hold on to the things of God.

10. If the same Spirit who raised Christ from the dead dwells in you, there is hope for every situation you will ever face.

- - - - - - - - - - - - - - - SECTION 8 - - - - - - - - - - - - - -

THE COMFORT OF GOD

I, even I, am He who comforts you.

— Isaiah 51:12

CHAPTER 50

GOD IS LOVE

The biblical view of God is that He is actively present in our lives because He cares. "God is love" is the clearest and most precise definition of God in the Bible. Love is the essence of who God is. God's love permeates every one of His thoughts and actions. He always has your best interest at heart. In particular, He keeps working with you so that you will come to know Him and learn to rely upon His love. Your healing and salvation come as you open your heart to His love. God's caring love is the heart of His relationship with His people.

Love is the essence of who God is.

The Truth of Scripture

(The Lord) heals the brokenhearted and binds up their wounds. (Psalm 147:3)

As a father has compassion on his children, so the Lord has compassion on those who fear him. (Psalm 103:13)

God is our refuge and strength, an ever present help in trouble. (Psalm 46:1)

As a mother comforts her child, so I will comfort you: (Isaiah 66:13)

Yet the Lord longs to be gracious to you; he rises to show you compassion. (Isaiah 30:18)

I have loved you with an everlasting love; I have drawn you with loving-kindness. (Jeremiah 31:3)

Because of God's great love we are not consumed, for his compassions never fail. They are new every morning; great is your faithfulness. (Lamentations 3:22, 23)

God is love. (I John 4:16)

Although you hurt badly at times, you can still believe that God is love. You can believe that He is moving through all your pain and sorrow to bring you into His peace. You can look to Him for strength to stand in the storms of life and grace to face your pain. He can give you faith to grieve your losses, courage to name your fears, and hope to meet your tomorrows. When you receive these gifts of grace as life unfolds, you can "know and rely on the love God has for us" (I John 4:16).

Knowing God as a comforting presence will help you deal with pain. He desires that you come to Him with your struggles. Because you are secure in His love, you can ask Him to join you in your trials. He knows your needs, and He cares about you. He desires to be with you through the hard and painful times. His presence will give you comfort and strength. God's caring presence is a miracle of His grace.

CHAPTER 51

GOD SEES YOU

A father told me a most heartwarming story. His wife had died suddenly following the birth of their second child. It was a time of shock and deep grief for both him and his seven-year-old son. One evening his son was in bed unable to go to sleep. Mother was not there to tuck him in. His heart was breaking as he cried for her. His dad heard him crying and went into his room to comfort him. They talked and cried together. When the father left, his son followed him and crawled into bed beside him. He did not want to be alone.

But he still could not go to sleep. Then, in the darkness, the son reached over to touch his father's face. "Dad," he said, "which way is your face turned?" The father's face was turned upward toward the ceiling. The son said, "Dad, if I know your face is turned toward me, I think I can go to sleep."

The father, with deep emotion, said to me, "As I turned my face toward my son so he could go to sleep, I became aware that my heavenly Father had turned His face toward me, and I, too, could go to sleep."

> **For he has not despised or disdained**
> **the suffering of the afflicted one;**
> **he has not hidden his face from him**
> **but has listened to his cry for help.**
> — Psalm 22:24

Hear my voice when I call, O Lord;
be merciful to me and answer me.
My heart says of you, "Seek his face!"
Your face, Lord, I will seek.

— Psalm 27:7, 8

In His love for you, God turns His face toward you and sees you in your struggles, griefs, and heartaches. At the cross, He turned to face the depths of your sin and despair. Even though we "hid, as it were, our faces from Him" (Isaiah 53:3 NKJV), He has not hidden His face from us. He is the God who sees you and knows your needs. The psalmist expresses the cry of our hearts: "Look upon me and be merciful to me" (Psalm 119:132, NKJV).

At the cross, Jesus turned to face
the depths of your sin and despair.

CHAPTER 52

HAGAR BY THE WELL

I especially love the Old Testament story of Abraham, Sarah, and Hagar, the handmaiden of Sarah. When Sarah could not bear children to Abraham, she gave Hagar to Abraham to bear a child, hoping to become a surrogate mother to Abraham's child and thus to build a family. Sarah believed that this plan would enable God to fulfill His promise to Abraham that he would be the father of many nations.

After Hagar became pregnant with Abraham's child, she became proud and arrogant toward Sarah (TLB). Sarah complained to Abraham that Hagar despised her now that she was pregnant with his child. The story says that Sarah dealt harshly with Hagar. In a moment of fear, Hagar fled into the desert to escape Sarah's wrath. She stopped by a spring to refresh herself. There an angel of the Lord ministered to her and told her to return to Sarah and submit herself to her.

Now hear this significant truth in the story: "She gave this name to the Lord who spoke to her: 'You are the God who sees me,' for she said, 'I have now seen the One who sees me'" (Genesis 16:13). The well from which Hagar refreshed herself is named Beer Lahai Roi which means "You Are The God Who Sees." Because she saw the God who sees her, she was able to return to a difficult place.

Charles Spurgeon wrote: "I looked at God and He looked at me, and we were one forever."

CHAPTER 53

SEE THE GOD WHO SEES YOU

One day I was holding my three-year-old granddaughter, Amber, while she was trying to talk to me. I was distracted elsewhere and not responding to her. She was patient for a little while, but finally she took my face in both her hands and turned it toward her to look into her eyes. "Pappy," she said, "you're not looking at me." My heart melted. I had not been paying attention. Now I looked and listened.

God desires that you turn your face to see Him. Sometimes, through suffering, He takes your face in His hands and turns you to look at Him. Job finally broke out of his despair when God turned Job's face toward Himself. Job said to the Lord, "My ears had heard of you, but now my eyes have seen you" (Job 42:5). Hagar was able to return to a difficult place and submit herself to a difficult mistress when she saw the One who sees her.

When you see the One who sees you, you will be strengthened. You will see the One who is the Mighty God, the Rock of Ages, the Prince of Peace, the Everlasting Father, the Comforter, the Healer of all your diseases. You will see the God of majesty and of power, the awesome Creator of all things, including you! In His love He sees you and turns your face to see Him. When you see the Lord, you are secure in His strength and grace, for you have now seen the One who knows you and loves you.

CHAPTER 54

GOD KNOWS WHERE YOU ARE

God sees your pain and brokenness. He knows where you are.

He sees your heartaches, disappointments, griefs, and sorrows. He knows where you are.

He sees your lostness, darkness, hopelessness, and fears. He knows where you are.

He sees your desperate attempts to save yourself. He knows where you are.

"I am the light of the world," He shouts into the dark places of your life. "I am come that you might have life and have it more abundantly. Come, follow Me."

Yes, you struggle, suffer, sin, and lose your way many times in life. But God knows where you are. You hurt, cry, protest, and become discouraged. But God knows where you are. Sometimes you want to give up. You lose the will to go on. You think that death would be a sweet release from pain. But God knows where you are and keeps coming to you with His comfort and hope. You may feel lost, but He always knows where you are.

To see God in all of His fulness—the God of love, the God of promise, the God of hope, the God of eternal life, God the present One—comforts you, for you have seen the One who sees you. In God, you are never alone and never without hope. Even when your spirit is crushed, your heart broken, and your prayers not answered as you had hoped,

God sees you and is with you. His love for you binds you inseparably to His heart.

**Christ's love for you binds you
inseparably to His heart.**

In Christ, the cross and the empty tomb become your life-giving hope. When you are lost, weary, or afraid, you come to Christ to draw the living water. You bring your pain and sorrow to the cross and to the empty tomb. They will stand forever as eternal wells of God's life-giving grace. In the shadow of the cross and by way of the empty tomb, you come to a personal and life-changing awareness:

GOD KNOWS WHERE YOU ARE!

CHAPTER 55

MOMENTS OF GRACE

There are special moments in which God chooses to comfort you with a touch of His grace. I call them "God moments." God speaks, He moves, and He comes swiftly to your aid. You are saved, healed, strengthened, renewed. And you know it is by the hand of God. There is just no other explanation.

Surely that was the experience of Hagar when God spoke to her in the wilderness and showed her a well. It was the grace in an angel's touch that woke a depressed Elijah and fed him. It was an angel who strengthened Jesus in the Garden when He was weary unto death. An angel spoke to Joseph in a dream and warned him of King Herod's intent to find the child Jesus to kill Him. It was an angel who rolled away the stone from the tomb of Jesus. An angel of the Lord loosed the chains that were holding Peter in jail and freed him.

**Watch for moments of grace to
sustain you through difficult times.**

The testimonies of countless thousands point to particular times at which they experienced the saving grace of an angel sent from God to minister to them. Sometimes it was to warn them of dangers, sometimes to lead them through difficult situations, sometimes to protect them from harm. Perhaps it was to deliver them from some evil or to encourage and comfort them in a stressful time. Whenever God personally intervened on their behalf, it became a moment of grace, hallowed by God's divine presence. Watch for moments of grace to sustain you through difficult times. They do happen!

In one of my most trying moments, God spoke to me through a nurse. She walked into a small treatment room in Miami Beach, Florida, where my daughter's newborn baby had just been examined by a pediatrician. The baby had been born with serious health problems. She cried and screamed as the pediatrician examined her. I was growing weary, and my nerves were frayed.

The nurse asked about the baby's condition. I told her everything that had been happening. First, the baby had begun having seizures shortly after her birth. Then my daughter herself had become critically ill and was admitted to the same hospital. Here I was trying to care for both of them in a strange city among strange people, driving around in a rented car. I was exhausted, running out of energy, apprehensive, broke, and very homesick. I didn't think that I could hold on much longer!

She listened attentively to me, asked some questions, and made some comments. As she was leaving, she turned and quietly said, "You know, when you are in trouble you can always call on the name of the Lord Jesus to help you."

"When you are in trouble you can always call on the name of the Lord Jesus to help you."

I stood to attention in the presence of the Lord! Strange feelings of awe and wonderment swept through my soul. Could this be an angel who had spoken to me at the point of my deepest need? It was exactly what I needed to hear. An angel or not, I was upheld by the grace of God.

That encounter, that word from the Lord, moved my heart from fear to confidence, from restlessness to peace, from self-pity to hope. In a moment my situation changed. Well, what really changed was me: my attitude, my spirit, my heart. The circumstances did not change. My perspective changed. "When you are in trouble you can always call on the name of the Lord Jesus to help you." Those words helped me to remember who I am in Christ and where my strength comes from. From that moment on, I refocused my spirit and became aware of God's presence.

I began to call on the name of the Lord Jesus. Every time my fears returned and my stomach rolled up in big, swirling knots, whether on a freeway in Miami battling the late afternoon traffic, flying through a storm in a plane, lost in a strange city among strange people, or waking up in a strange place in the still of the night, I would whisper the name of the Lord Jesus and my spirit would become calm. Speaking His name brought peace to my heart.

**Speaking the name of Jesus will
bring peace to your heart.**

I made it home safely and in sound mind by God's grace. I discovered the truth of the words of the Apostle Paul: "For he himself is our peace" (Ephesians 2:14). One word from the Lord can change your moment and can also change you.

> In the very thought of Jesus,
>   His presence can be found.
> He's as close as the mention of His name.

There is never any distance
    between my Lord and me,
He's as close as the mention of His name.

In my hour of struggle
    so many times I've found,
He's as close as the mention of His name.
Just to breathe the Name of Jesus
    can turn everything around,
He's as close as the mention of His name.[19]

— Gordon Jensen

PRINCIPLES

1. Love is the essence of who God is.

2. You can "know and rely on the love God has for you."

3. At the cross, Jesus faced the depths of your sins and despair.

4. God knows where you are and sees you in your need.

5. The cross and the empty tomb become your life-giving hope.

6. Speaking the name of Jesus will bring peace to your heart.

7. Watch for moments of grace to sustain you through difficult times.

8. "When you are in trouble you can always call on the name of the Lord Jesus to help you."

9. One word from the Lord will change your moment and will also change you.

‐ ‐ ‐ ‐ ‐ ‐ ‐ ‐ ‐ ‐ ‐ ‐ ‐ **SECTION 9** ‐ ‐ ‐ ‐ ‐ ‐ ‐ ‐ ‐ ‐ ‐ ‐ ‐

ABIDING IN GOD'S LOVE

Abide in My love.
— John 15:9 (NKJV)

CHAPTER 56

THE GOD WHO COMFORTS

I was stunned! I couldn't believe what I was hearing. Our pediatrician was telling my wife Sandy and me that our five-year-old son Steve had a serious heart murmur. He had been doing very well. There had been no health problems. Sandy and I left the doctor's office in a daze. Had we heard him correctly? What was going on here? It couldn't be!

Steve was hospitalized and checked out by specialists. No one could diagnose his problem, so he was scheduled for more tests at Children's Hospital in Pittsburgh. A heart catheterization revealed that he had been born with a congenital defect known as anomalous origin of the left coronary from the pulmonary artery. He was scheduled for major surgery. The cardiologists were amazed that he had survived to this point without major heart damage. His chances of having survived without heart damage were set at one tenth of one percent. The cardiologists and surgeons hoped to correct his genetic condition by a new type of surgical procedure.

It was a traumatic time for me. At first I felt dazed and disoriented. I couldn't believe this was happening to us. Then I began my protest. "This isn't right, God," I cried. "Steve did nothing to deserve this. He is such a precious child. And, furthermore, I've been trying to serve You as a hardworking pastor. Is this the reward I get? Is this how You treat Your people? Your pastors?"

Then I went through stages of guilt. What had I done to deserve this? Oh, yes, I could think of many sins in my life. I thought of the times I had acted in selfish ways and all the times I had shortchanged God. Yes, I could see why I deserved this pain. "All have sinned." "There is none righteous, no, not one." I could see that I deserved to be punished. I was no better than anyone else. But why take it out on my son? "God, if You have a bone to pick with me, come and get me," I challenged Him one night as I thumped on my chest with my finger. "Take it out on me. Not my son! Please, not my precious son!"

Then I began to seek God with my whole heart. I prayed and fasted. I pled with God for Steve's healing. I applied all the scriptures of promise and healing I could find. I hovered between hope and despair. One moment I had peace that all would be well. Another time I would imagine the worst possible outcome. It was a very anxious and painful time.

With great difficulty, I continued my work as a pastor. Sometimes I would stop and cry between pastoral visits. Or I'd put on a brave face and lead a memorial service. I would dedicate babies to the "honor and glory of God" and pray for their health and safety. I would hold onto both sides of the pulpit as I tried to preach. Pastoral prayers were the most difficult for me. At those times I brought the joys and pains, fears and hopes of the congregation before God. Sometimes I just cried as I prayed. It was the only honest expression of my heart at that particular moment.

I felt guilty for not being stronger in my faith. "I must be strong for my people," I would often say to myself. "They have many hurts, too. I can't falter as their pastor." How many times I had encouraged families to exercise their faith and trust in God at such times. Surely God would hear their prayers and heal their loved ones. If not, He would be with them and see them through. After all, we were all heading to a better place. How glibly and carelessly I had often spoken those words. Now it was my turn to hope, to pray, to cry, to be confused and anxious, to wait.

The night before Steve's surgery, I drove out into the mountains to pray and to be alone with God. I climbed a fire tower to get as close to heaven as possible. At the top of the tower I cried out for my son's healing. I determined not to leave until I had found peace with God. It was my time of wrestling with God all night.

I found peace that night. There were no flashing lights or angelic visits. My peace came in the quietness of the Holy Spirit, who called my attention to a teaching of Christ about an earthly father and a heavenly Father. He taught that if an earthly father knows how to give good gifts to his children, how much more the Father in heaven will give all good things to those who ask Him (Matthew 7:9-11).

I began to understand my heavenly Father's love in a new way. I loved Steve to the point that I had become one with him in his suffering. My whole being ached for his healing. I would have gladly taken his place on the operating table. I wanted so much for him to live and to be whole.

Then the truth of my heavenly Father's love hit home. If I loved my son in my own imperfect, earthly way, how much more did the heavenly Father love Steve in His own perfect, heavenly way? I saw that God loved my son more than I could ever love him. That truth swept through me like a soft, cooling breeze on a hot, stormy night. It began to comfort me.

**If you, then, though you are evil, know how
to give good gifts to your children, how much more
will your Father in heaven give good gifts to those
who ask him!**

—Matthew 7:11

I saw yet another life-changing truth that night. The heavenly Father loved me, too! He loved me more than I could ever love my own son. I knew how much I loved my son. I had told God that I was willing to lay down my life for him. Now I came to see how much God loved me. I saw the great truth that God, who truly and perfectly loved His Son, had already laid down the life of His beloved Son that I might live!

**He who did not spare his own Son,
    but gave him up for us all—
how will he not also,
    along with him,
graciously give us all things?**

— Romans 8:32

I stood on that fire tower in awe of this new revelation of God's love. If God loved my son more than I could ever love him, then surely He would be watching over him and caring for him. In my newfound knowledge, I was able to release Steve into the care of his heavenly Father. As this revelation began to comfort my spirit and give me hope, I was able to release my fears. That night I left the mountains in peace. Now I could rest in my Father's love. The greatest miracle of life is to come to know God's love and to be forever changed by that experience. Indeed, " . . . perfect love casts out fear" (I John 4:18, NKJV).

Steve experienced many touches of God's healing as he went through his surgery and recovery. Later, as a senior in high school, he was the lead runner for his cross-country team. God gave him special gifts that he is now using in the health profession. I praise God every day for His miracle of grace in Steve's life.

My heart goes out to the many families whose stories have ended differently. Another child who had heart surgery at the same time did not survive his first year. One day he collapsed and died while in school. He had been doing very well. I do not understand nor can I explain why some people experience healing and others do not. I only know that you and I live in God's grace every day.

In the midst of unanswered questions, an understanding of God's love brings a healing perspective to your pain. God's love absorbs the shocks and bruises along the way. A personal relationship with God will relieve many of your fears, for "God is love" (I John 4:8, 16). His love offers you comfort and security in the midst of pain. God seeks you during painful times and desires to draw you close to His heart so that you will come to know Him and abide in His love. There is comfort in His love.

"I, even I, am he who comforts you" (Isaiah 51:12).

**God's love offers you comfort and
security in the midst of pain.**

CHAPTER 57

"DON'T BE SAD, I LOVE YOU"

My granddaughter Amber and I sat on the floor one evening drawing pictures. Suddenly she said, "Let's draw a picture of Rocky." Our poodle, Rocky, had been our family pet for many years. Just recently, he had died. We were all feeling Rocky's loss. In particular, I especially missed my long evening walks with him when I would take him out for our "walkie-talkies." Amber's desire to draw a picture of him was her way of expressing our loss.

I replied to Amber, "I'm very sad. I really miss Rocky. He's the best dog we ever had."

She was silent for a monent, and then she looked up at me and said so tenderly, "Don't be sad, Pappy. I love you."

"Don't be sad, I love you" is the tender expression of God to you when you are hurting. When you are sad, when you have lost that which was the most precious to you, He desires to draw you near to Him to comfort you with His love.

Learning to trust in God's love is your greatest need as well as your most difficult struggle. To let God love you when you are hurting is the most comforting thing you can do. You let go of your fears and rest in God's love. You relinquish your disappointments, your pains, and your sorrows into God's love. You lay them down at the feet of Jesus and simply trust in Him. You come to know the love of Christ that the Apostle Paul describes:

And I pray that you, being rooted and established in love, may have power, together with all the saints, to grasp how wide and long and high and deep is the love of Christ, and to know this love that surpasses knowledge—that you may be filled to the measure of all the fullness of God.

— Ephesians 3:17-19

CHAPTER 58

REVEALED IN CHRIST

"God is love" (I John 4: 8, 16) is the clearest and most precise biblical definition of God. The heart of His thoughts, actions, and plans for His creation is love. You will never come to know or understand how God works in your life until you have accepted this basic revelation that "God is love." Everything in life depends upon God's love for you.

God's love is a truth that must be revealed to you. You cannot grasp it through your physical knowledge, senses, or experiences. It is a spiritual truth that has been revealed in Christ. In Christ, you see God's love expressed in real life. When Philip asked Jesus to show him the Father, Jesus said: "Anyone who has seen me has seen the Father. . . . it is the Father, living in me, who is doing his work" (John 14:9, 10). God's love is revealed in Christ.

Divine love is not something you make happen. It is something divine which happens to you. It is not something you grasp. It grasps you. It is a revelation of God. It is the true expression of the nature and purpose of God. The essence of God is love. The Apostle John is so very clear on how you come to know God's love: "This is how we know what love is: Jesus Christ laid down his life for us" (I John 3:16).

This is how God showed His love among us:
He sent his one and only Son into the world that
we might live through him. This is love: not that

**we loved God, but that he loved us and sent his
Son as an atoning sacrifice for our sins.**
—I John 4:9, 10

One day I received a picture of Christ stretched out on the cross. The caption beneath the picture read: "I asked Jesus how much He loved me. He stretched out His arms and said, 'This much'—and died."

When you receive Christ by faith, you come into the Father's love. Jesus said that he who receives the Son receives the Father who sent Him. Faith believes that God revealed Himself through His special Son, Jesus Christ, and that His revelation is true. The Apostle Paul wrote: "Here is a trustworthy saying that deserves full acceptance: Christ Jesus came into the world to save sinners . . ." (I Timothy 1:15).

Christ is the revelation of God's love. The revelation of Christ is received by faith. It is a trustworthy revelation because Christ came from the Father to be Truth. He is the Truth in whom you can believe and base your life upon. You come to know God's love when you open your heart to His Son, seek Him with your whole heart, and receive by faith the merits of His wonderful grace.

CHAPTER 59

A GIFT OF HIS GRACE

Faith is a gift of God. You cannot believe in God or in His Son without the gift of faith. The ability to trust in God's love is a gift of His grace. You cannot trust in God by your own knowledge or by your own will. To believe, you need a faith that is given to you from above. You need the Holy Spirit—the Spirit of Truth—to dwell within you. The coming and indwelling of the Holy Spirit is an act of God's power and grace. The Holy Spirit is the Spirit of Truth who reveals truth to the human heart. He teaches you all things, reveals Christ to you, convicts you of sin and righteousness, and reminds you of the words of Christ. The Holy Spirit is the faith generator who has been implanted into your spirit by God.

There have been times—painful times—when I tried again and again to trust God and surrender my needs into His care. I brought Him my painful situations and prayed prayers of relinquishment only to be haunted by them again. I cried out, "God, is there no relief? I have given You this pain. I have acknowledged my fears. I have confessed my need of You. You know my weaknesses. You have promised to be with me, to comfort me. Yet I am still lonely, hurting, and afraid. I cannot bear this burden any longer. I need You! Please help me!"

Slowly and painfully I come to realize that trusting in God's love is beyond my own doing. As hard as I try, I cannot make it happen. God's love is so far beyond anything else I have ever experienced. I simply cannot comprehend it. I must surrender my need to be loved into God's grace. My prayer is that God's love will apprehend me and be released in me. That is my hope! I ask Him to grant me the gift of faith so I can believe. I ask Him to fill me with His Holy Spirit so that I can see truth. Jesus said you can ask the Father and He will give the Holy Spirit to you (Luke 11:13). The Holy Spirit reveals the truth of God to you, and you are comforted by that revelation.

CHAPTER 60
RECEIVED BY FAITH

You do not deserve it, you do not comprehend it, you may not know how to live by it, but it is here for you now and forever—the love of God. God's love is received by faith in Christ. Faith in Christ comes as you open your heart to receive Him. Faith is accepting what God is offering in Christ. It is believing that what is revealed in Christ is true and trustworthy. By the witness of the Holy Spirit, you are invited to believe, receive, and live your life in this truth.

Living in the truth revealed in Christ is not a matter of understanding; it's a matter of believing. It's not a matter of explaining; it's a matter of receiving. It's not a matter of trying; it's a matter of living by faith. "Seeing is believing" is the accepted norm of the world. In the Christian faith, "believing is seeing."

> Faith is not understanding; it's believing.
> Faith is not explaining; it's receiving.
> Faith is not trying; it's living.

Your struggle to find God and rest in His love begins with your sense of pain and alienation. Then, driven by pain, you turn to Him, acknowledge your sin and brokenness, confess your faithlessness, and ask Him to increase your faith so that you might come to rely upon His love. Recognition, confession, and turning from self to seek God lie at the very heart of knowing Him. God is there for you to know. God is there to love you and for you to love Him.

God is there for you to rest in. He is there to comfort you. He promises that those who seek Him diligently will find Him (Hebrews 11:6). To know Him is to love Him, and to love Him is to know Him.

> **God is love. Whoever lives in love**
> **lives in God, and God in him.**
> — I John 4:16

CHAPTER 61

TO BE REVEALED

Although we are constantly surrounded by God's love on this earth, we gain only glimpses of that love. As the Apostle Paul said, "Now we see but a poor reflection as in a mirror; then we shall see face to face. Now I know in part; then I shall know fully, even as I am fully known" (I Corinthians 13:12). The best is yet to come! The full revelation of God's love will be revealed when He gathers His people home to be with Him. The Apostle Paul quotes from Isaiah the prophet: " 'No eye has seen, no ear has heard, no mind has conceived what God has prepared for those who love him'—but God has revealed it to us by his Spirit" (I Corinthians 2:9, 10).

Your life of faith in Christ will come into complete rest and fulfillment in heaven. Your greatest joy will be oneness with the Father, the Son, and the Holy Spirit. The One you were not able to see fully on your journey of faith, yet whose presence you knew, will be seen in His full glory! You will know the fulness of the Father's love at last!

In your new home, you will be one with Christ. He will receive you fully into His love. The nailprints in His hands and feet will be vivid reminders of His great love. Only then will you comprehend the depth of His love for you. You will worship at His feet in great joy and thankfulness. As you sit at His feet, He will tell you the meaning of all the things that happened on this earth. Then you will understand the meaning of your pain and sorrows. You will understand how God worked in your life to bring you into His plan. You will be astounded at how He worked to bring about His will in your life and then lead you home. Yes, "Jesus led me all the way." All your protests and questions will have answers. You will understand. It will be a great time of oneness, understanding, healing, praise, and completeness. Oh, to know the fulness of His love! Oh, to be home!

In heaven, all your longings will be fulfilled. There will be no sorrow. No night. All your pain will be healed in the loving presence of God. All your tears will be redeemed by Christ's love. The scars of sin will be healed. The meaning of your life will be understood in God's eternal plan of salvation. You will be at peace, finally at peace. Home at last! You have this hope, and so you press on. The day of salvation is at hand. Hold on, my brother. Press on, my sister. Joy comes in the morning!

Corrie ten Boom wrote words of hope that were forged by her suffering:

> The best is yet to be. What a comfort! When things become difficult and frightening, just read the last page of the Bible. Yes, the best is yet to be! And the sufferings of this present time cannot be compared to the joys of the time that is coming. What a comfort that is![20]

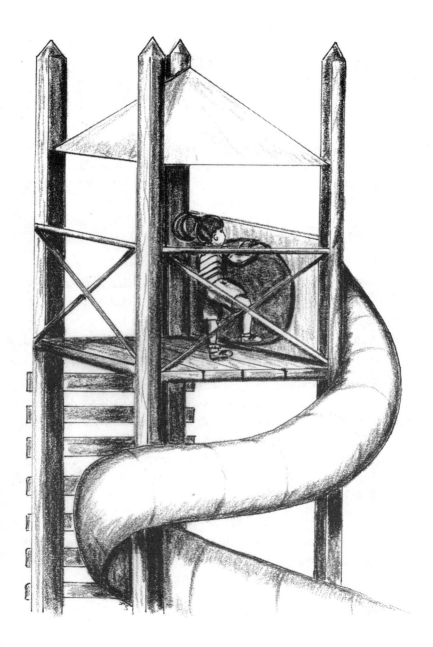

CHAPTER 62

TRUSTING GOD AND LETTING GO

Our precious granddaughter Amber, at the age of four, taught me an important lesson about trust one day. Sandy and I were with her on a beach at a state park in western Pennsylvania. She was having a good time running in the water, playing on the beach, digging holes, filling them with water, and then watching the water flow back into the lake.

All of a sudden I looked around for her and she was gone. A panicky feeling came over me. I did a quick scan of the area. There she was, running up the beach, her long, black hair flowing in the breeze. Her little legs moved faster than mine as I made an effort to catch up with her.

She was heading toward a play area up the beach where a gym set with long, winding steps led upward to different tiers. At the top was the head of a tubular sliding board that circled down around the set and emptied onto the beach. By the time I got there, she was standing at the very top looking down into the slide. I knew what she had in mind. She was coming down the slide!

I ran to the bottom of the slide to catch her. I stood there in silence, waiting intently. Soon she yelled down through the tube:

"Pappy, are you down there?"

"Yes, Amber, I'm here."

"Are you going to catch me?"

"Yes, I'll catch you. I'm here waiting for you."

There was a long silence. I could imagine what she was thinking. It was much higher than she had thought. It looked scary from the top. All she could see was a long tube winding downward into the darkness. She had never been in this position before. But she was not about to turn and walk back down those steps. Not Amber!

Then I heard her coming! And she was moving! I heard this swishing sound as she slid around the bends. She was gathering speed, and then—one final swish and—pop! She shot out of the darkness into my outstretched, waiting arms. I braced myself and held on!

She looked at me with her big, dark eyes wide open in surprise. "Pappy," she said, "you was there!" For a moment we were one in wonder and awe. Yes, I was there!

Amber had to let go and trust me. When she said in surprise "You was there!", I realized how much courage it had taken for her to let go and to trust me. She let herself slide into the darkness not seeing what lay ahead, hearing only my voice. I had earned her trust by being there for her many times in other situations. But she had never faced one quite like this before. It was me she trusted! The voice of a stranger she would not have trusted.

In your relationship with God, you come to places and situations in which you have never been before. You can't turn back. You don't know what God will do. He tells you to let go and to trust Him. You look down the dark corridor and see no one. It's a plunge of faith. You let go, often because you have no choice. Life pushes you on. Swish! You are on a journey you never took before. It's dark and scary.

But God is waiting there to catch you, to bear you up. You are surprised to find Him waiting for you. He knows where you are, and He knows your needs. If Amber could trust me, an imperfect grandpa, how much more can you trust God, your strong and perfect heavenly Father, to be there for you! He knows your needs and loves you with an everlasting love. He is the One you can trust!

Leslie Williams, in her book *Night Wrestling*, writes that ". . . there is no such thing as a Christian tragedy because, though tragic things may happen . . . the Christian always ends up in the arms of God."[21]

"The eternal God is your refuge, and underneath are the everlasting arms." (Deuteronomy 33:27)

Daily you are called to let go of the things of this life to take hold of God. You lay down many unfulfilled dreams and longings of the heart as you move along. You experience many losses. You are called to bear many burdens and suffer through many griefs and sorrows. Life is tough. But the many times you have experienced the trustworthiness of God prepare you to trust Him again and again as you encounter new things. And, ultimately, you are called to trust Him with your very life as you say with Christ, "Father, into Your hands I commit my spirit." The little relinquishments you are called to make in this life prepare you for your final "letting go and trusting God." You can only receive what God has for you as you let go of the desires of this world in order to take hold of Him. The hard knocks of life teach you to attach yourself to God. He is the way through the darkness. And He is also your final destination. All your life you are heading toward Him. He is your Home.

CHAPTER 63

ALMOST HOME

I remember so well the long trips in the family station wagon when our children were young. It didn't take long until they became restless. The way to Pittsburgh was long and hard. They had a goal in mind: grandpa and grandma's house, but it just took too long to get there. Again and again they would ask, "Are we there yet?" Often I would answer, "We're not there yet, but we're on the way. We'll soon be there."

And, of course, there was the return trip. They were always relieved to head back home. We just couldn't get there fast enough!

"Dad, are we almost home?"

"Not yet, but we're moving in the right direction."

"How long will it take?"

"A while. You'll have to be patient."

"But, dad, it's hot back here. Can't you go faster?"

"I can't go much faster. But we're heading in the right direction. We'll soon be there. Be patient just a little longer."

"Dad, are we there yet?"

Soon they fell asleep in the faith that mom and dad would get them safely home.

When we arrived home, Sandy and I would gather them carefully into our arms, carry them inside, and tuck them into bed. They would wake up in the morning at home and refreshed.

Yes, you are almost Home, my friend, almost Home. Hold on a little longer! The Father is in charge, and you can rest. In that faith you are free on this earth to pour out your heart of love for Christ. He has something for you that only you can do. Serve Him on the journey Home. Serve Him with great joy! Make this world a better place while you are here. Love God with your whole heart and serve others in the spirit of Christ.

Be patient! Hold on! You will soon be Home! When it's your time to fall asleep, He will gather you tenderly into His arms and carry you home. You will awaken in the morning new and refreshed. You will finally be Home. The journey will be worth it all when we see Jesus!

> Through many dangers, toils and snares,
>   I have already come;
> 'Tis grace that brought me safe thus far,
>   And grace will lead me home.
>   — John Newton

CONCLUSION

PERSONAL AFFIRMATION OF FAITH

Life hurts. God is love.

Pain is real. God is eternal.

Life is tough. God is good.

I cannot change anything that has happened to me. But God will give me the strength to deal with it and the grace to go on.

I cannot prevent bad things from happening to me. But God has promised to be with me in the dark times of my life.

I do not understand or appreciate pain. But God can use those experiences in my life to draw me closer to Him.

I do not understand why bad things happen to good people. But I believe that God can work things out for good for those who love Him and are called according to His purpose.

I do not understand the meaning and the purpose of pain. But I can look for grace to the One who bore my pain and carried my sorrows in His body on the Tree.

I have a lot of questions about why God allows so much suffering in the world. But I believe in the goodness of God.

I may ask where God is when life hurts. But I believe His promise that He will be with me always, even to the end of the age.

I do not understand the nature of evil. But I believe that good will overcome evil.

I do not understand why I must suffer and will die someday. But I believe that God will fulfill His promise to come for me so that where He is I may be also.

I do not understand death. But I believe that Christ is the Resurrection and the Life.

I do not understand why the journey is so long and hard. But I believe the journey will be fulfilled in the presence of God.

I will never come to understand or appreciate pain. But I know that God's love will sustain me through the painful times.

In the midst of my pain, I can trust in God's ultimate promise of healing. I can rest in His love and goodness. I can believe in His love and care. I can rely on the love of God through Jesus Christ my Lord.

In that faith, I can look up, believe, and live! In that faith, I can go on day by day, placing my hope in the living God, trusting that the God who has been faithful to me in life will be faithful to me in eternal life, and believing that He will be with me all the way Home.

> **Who shall separate us
> from the love of Christ?
> Shall trouble
> or hardship
> or persecution. . . ?
> No, in all these things
> we are more than conquerors
> through him who loved us.**

206 @ Tears In a Bottle

**For I am convinced that . . .
(nothing) in all creation will be
able to separate us from the love of
God that is in Christ Jesus our Lord.**
— Romans 8:35-39

PRINCIPLES

---

1. God is love.

2. The greatest miracle is to know God's love and to be forever changed by it.

3. God's love absorbs the shocks and bruises along the way.

4. In Christ, you see God's love expressed in real life.

5. Faith is a gift of God.

6. The fulness of God's love is yet to be revealed.

7. The sufferings of this present time cannot be compared to the joys that await you.

8. The Christian always ends up in the arms of God.

9. Life is tough, but God is good.

10. Nothing can separate you from the love of God which is in Christ Jesus your Lord.

ENDNOTES

Chapter 2

1. Dr. Paul Brand & Philip Yancey, *Pain: The Gift Nobody Wants* (New York: HarperCollins, 1993), p. 197.

Chapter 3

2. Tom Lutz, *Crying: The Natural and Cultural History of Tears* (New York: W. W. Norton & Co., 1999), p. 17.

3. Granger E. Westberg, *Good Grief* (Philadelphia: Fortress Press, 1971), p. 64.

Chapter 7

4. Tim Hansel, *You Gotta Keep Dancin'* (Colorado Springs: Victor Books, 1985), p. 123

Chapter 11

5. Philip Yancey, *Disappointment with God* (Grand Rapids: Zondervan Publishing House, 1988), p. 284.

Chapter 12

6. Tim Hansel, *You Gotta Keep Dancin'*, p. 42.

Chapter 15

7. Elie Wiesel, *Night* (New York: Bantam Books, 1960), p. 32.

8. Ibid., p. 62.

9. Corrie ten Boom, *Not I, But Christ* (Nashville: Thomas Nelson Publishers, 1983), p. 44.

10. Ibid., p. 61.

Chapter 23

11. Philip Yancey, *Where Is God When It Hurts?* (New York: HarperPaperbacks, 1990), p. 206.

Chapter 24

12. "He's Still in the Fire" by Tim Hill. © Copyright 1989. My Father's House/BMI (adm. by IGG). All Rights Reserved. Used by permission.

Chapter 28

13. Ken Gire, *Incredible Moments With the Savior* (Grand Rapids: Zondervan Publishing House, 1990), pp. 96-97.

Chapter 29

14. Philip Yancey, *Where Is God When It Hurts?,* p. 207.

Chapter 40

15. Carman, Mission 3:16, "We Are Not Ashamed", Sparrow Communication Group, P.O. Box 5010, Brentwood TN 37024.

Chapter 41

16. Patsy Clairmont, *Under His Wings and Other Places of Refuge* (Colorado Springs: Focus on the Family) Copyright @ 1994 by Patsy Clairmont, pp. 140-141.

Chapter 48

17. Elisabeth Elliot, *A Lamp For My Feet* (Ann Arbor: Servant Books, 1985), p. 32.

Chapter 49

18. Eileen Egan and Kathleen Egan, OSB, *Suffering Into Joy* (Ann Arbor: Servant Publications, *1994), p. 118.*

Chapter 55

19. "He's As Close As the Mention of His Name" by Gorden Jensen. Copyright © 1978 by Jensen Music/ASCAP. International Copyright secured. All rights controlled by The Benson Co., Inc.

Chapter 61

20. Corrie ten Boom, *Not I, But Christ*, p. 102.

Chapter 62

21. Leslie Williams, *Night Wrestling* (Dallas: Word Publishing, 1997), p. 98.

COPYRIGHT PERMISSION NOTICES

ABOUT THE AUTHOR

NOAH S. MARTIN, D.Min. serves as a pastor, a marriage and family therapist, and an author. He is a Clinical Member of the American Association for Marriage and Family Therapy and a Charter Member of the American Association for Christian Counselors. He is an ordained minister in the Church of the Brethren.

Noah has dedicated his life to helping people deal with difficult situations. In 1978, after serving as a pastor for eleven years, he began a Christian ministry for at-risk youth and families called New Day, Inc. which he serves as Executive Director. His efforts have helped to establish Christian ministries to at-risk youth and families and professional and lay Christian counseling centers in westcentral Pennsylvania and other areas.

Noah and his wife, Sandra, live in Johnstown, Pennsylvania. They are the parents of four children and the grandparents of three granddaughters.